CASE STUDIES IN
CULTURAL ANTHROPOLOGY

GENERAL EDITORS

George and Louise Spindler

STANFORD UNIVERSITY

VASILIKA
A Village in Modern Greece

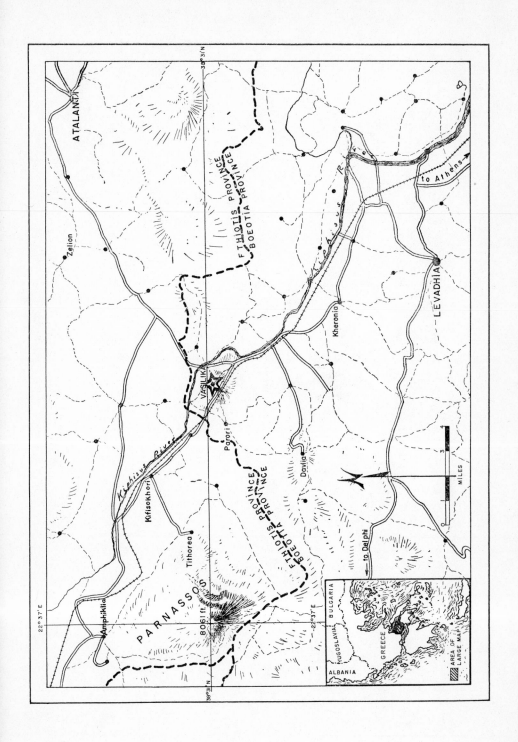

VASILIKA

A Village in Modern Greece

BY

ERNESTINE FRIEDL

Queens College

HOLT, RINEHART AND WINSTON · NEW YORK

Στοὺς ἀξέχαστούς μας φίλους,
τοὺς κατοίκους τῶν Βασιλικῶν,
μὲ ἀγάπη καὶ ἐκτίμηση.

*To our unforgettable friends,
the residents of Vasilika,
with affection and esteem.*

About the Series

THESE CASE studies in cultural anthropology are designed to bring to students, in beginning and intermediate courses in the social sciences, insights into the richness and complexity of human life as it is lived in different ways and in different places. They are written by men and women who have lived in the societies they write about, and who are professionally trained as observers and interpreters of human behavior. The authors are also teachers, and in writing their books they have kept the students who will read them foremost in their minds. It is our belief that when an understanding of ways of life very different from one's own is gained, abstractions and generalizations about social structure, cultural values, subsistence techniques, and the other universal categories of human social behavior become meaningful.

About the Author

Ernestine Friedl is associate professor of anthropology and sociology at Queens College in New York. She holds the Ph.D. in anthropology from Columbia University. Before coming to Queens, she taught at Wellesley College and at Brooklyn College. She has done field work among the Chippewa Indians of northern Wisconsin, and has published material on that tribe. Her field work in Greece was done in 1955-1956 and has resulted in several articles for professional journals as well as this book. Dr. Friedl has served as secretary-treasurer of the American Ethnological Society and is a fellow of the American Association for the Advancement of Science.

About the Book

Life in Vasilika has a flavor of its own. As Dr. Friedl points out in the introduction, one has two reactions in viewing this way of life for the first time—a strong sense of its familiarity and a surprised awareness of its strangeness. In the exploitation of these two dimensions, she has given us a compelling and intellectually satisfying analysis of a village in a contemporary national society that has ancient historic roots.

In this book the author makes one concrete part of life flow into another—from land resources to cotton cultivation, division of labor, concepts of cleanliness and order, the furnishing of homes, the dowry system, the ceremonies and festivities. And everywhere the evaluations that the people of Vasilika place upon these parts of life are made clear. In this way a patterned way of life as a whole emerges, and the reader learns about what the people do, and with what resources, at the same time he is learning about what the people think and feel about what they do.

We acquire insight into the quality of interpersonal relationships in Vasilika, which are like those between man and nature. Both are characterized by constant struggle. The individual is sustained and revitalized for this struggle within the family, and the struggle itself is a means of maintaining the identity of the self and of society.

GEORGE AND LOUISE SPINDLER
General Editors

Stanford, California
1962

Preface and Acknowledgments

THE FIELD WORK on which this book is based was conducted largely in 1955-1956 under a Fulbright grant, with supplementary funds from the Wenner-Gren Foundation for Anthropological Research. I am very grateful for this assistance. Return visits were made to the village for several weeks in the summer of 1959, and for two days in July 1961.

Margaret Mead and Hortense Powdermaker were most generous with their time during the initial stages of the project. In Greece, John Caskey, Peter and Eva Topping, Eurydice Demetracopoulou, Korali Krokodilou, and Olympias Kokkevi gave valuable advice, assistance, and encouragement.

John Melios, Nomarch of Boeotia at the time we resided there, helped in selecting the village and introduced my husband and me to the villagers. Our gratitude to him is very great both for this initial help and for his continued interest. Our thanks go also to K. Chlimintzas of the Agricultural Bank of Greece in Levadhia.

The family of Athanasius T. Triantaphyllou, who took us into their home in Vasilika, put us greatly in their debt for many kindly services besides.

Discussions with many scholars have contributed much to this book, though of course I bear sole responsibility for the points of view presented. I should like to mention Henry and Renee Kahane, Sidney Axelrad and Sylvia Brody, and John Andromedas, Fred Gearing, Popie Mohring, Irwin T. Sanders, and Conrad Arensberg.

My participation in the Wenner-Gren Conference on Rural Peoples of the Mediterranean at Burg Wartenstein, Austria, in 1959, and in the similar conference at the Athenian Social Science Center in Athens in 1961, helped me greatly. Special thanks are due to Julian Pitt-Rivers and to John Peristiany, the organizers of the two conferences.

To John Peristiany I am indebted also for his stimulating analysis of his own Greek field materials; John Campbell's treatment of data from his study of a Greek shepherd community was similarly illuminating.

For technical assistance of a high order, I am obliged to Robert E. Logan and to John Berthelsen.

Dorothy Demetracopoulou Lee, Kimon Lolos, and Ivan Paneras read an earlier draft of this manuscript and offered many helpful suggestions; to them I offer my best thanks.

My husband, Harry L. Levy, professor of classics and dean of students at Hunter College in the Bronx, deserves special mention. He is the other member of "we" when that pronoun is used in this volume. He participated in all the field work. His knowledge of the Greek language, both ancient and modern, has been an unfailing resource. His insights have provided clues to much of the life in the village. His editorial assistance has been invaluable. In truth, the book could not have been written without him.

E. F.

New York City
1962

Contents

VASILIKA

A Village in Modern Greece

Vasilika with Parori and Mt. Parnassos in the background.

Women hoeing.

Roasting the paschal lamb.

A woman of the village.

A young girl of the village.

Introduction

THE WAY OF LIFE of a rural village in modern Greece exists in a setting significantly different from that of the cultures and societies anthropologists have been accustomed to study. Cultural and social anthropologists traditionally have concentrated their professional interests on what are usually called the primitive peoples of the world. These include the Indians of North and South America, the Eskimo, the indigenous populations of Africa south of the Sahara, of Australia, and of the islands of the Pacific. What all these peoples had in common was not crudeness or inferiority; nor were they necessarily at the beginning stages of human cultural evolution, as the Latin root of the word "primitive" would suggest.

By the fifteenth century, when European explorations began in earnest, many of these primitive peoples had long since developed assured food supplies through the domestication of plants and animals, and had densely populated, complex stratified societies with sophisticated cosmologies and art styles. The Maya of Yucatan had conceived the mathematical concept of the zero, and both they and the Aztecs of Mexico had a rudimentary system of writing. But whether the primitive people were simple hunting and gathering populations who depended on wild foods, or whether they were pastoralists using their flocks for subsistence and for products to trade, or whether they were the sophisticated West Africans or Incas, the characteristic that they all had in common and that lay at the base of what was called their "primitiveness" was the fact that the cultures of these peoples had received no significant recent influences from either of the two early centers of cultural development on the Eurasiatic continent.

One of these centers was the Near East, where it appears that seed grasses such as wheat and barley were first domesticated, and where sheep, goats, and cattle were first controlled by men. The techniques for raising and cultivating these plants and animals spread south to Egypt, east to India, and west to Europe, where they furnished the original subsistence base for the development of the Egyptian, Hindu, and ancient Greek and Roman cultures. North China

1

was a second center where similar plants and animals were domesticated. Whether the Chinese subsistence base diffused directly from the Near East, or whether it is at least partly a separate development is not yet clear from the archeological evidence. In any case, the new techniques served as the subsistence base for the development of Far Eastern civilization. Some four thousand years ago systems of writing were invented in both these centers: the alphabet in the Near East and the logograph in the Far East. These systems spread in different directions but had not yet reached the American Indians, the Eskimo, the Africans south of the Sahara, the Australians, or the Pacific islanders by the time of the first European explorations.

For many primitive societies, then, the subsistence base was different from that of the Old World. In the New World, the more complex societies depended on different groups of domesticated plants and animals, on maize rather than wheat, for example, and on the llama and the alpaca, rather than cattle. Further, with the exception of the Maya and the Aztecs, the primitive peoples had developed no writing systems of their own. Nor did these peoples participate in the major world religions that had developed in the course of the last four thousand years of Eurasiatic history and that eventually depended upon sacred and semisacred written texts. With few exceptions the religions of the primitive peoples were derived neither from the Judaeo-Christian and Islamic traditions nor from the Hindu-Buddhist, Taoist, or Confucian.

Because European and American scholars were deeply steeped in the origins, history, and contemporary patterns of their own cultures, for them the main value of the study of the primitive peoples lay in the contrasts they provided with the ancient and modern variations of the way of life derived from the Near East.

The different historical provenience of the cultures of the American Indians, the Polynesians, and the rest made them exotic and interesting and, at the same time, gave to European scholars a natural laboratory of human cultural variation in which to test generalizations and hypotheses largely derived from analyzing the written records of their own tradition. Whenever cultural forms or social structures among the primitive peoples were similar to those known in the European tradition, some form of explanation other than similar historical derivation had to be found. In addition, the efforts to reconstruct the history of primitive societies and cultures and to analyze their contemporary functioning led to the formulation of new hypotheses concerning the history and evolution of cultures and societies in general, and concerning the nature of man himself.

In the last two decades many cultural anthropologists have turned to the study of societies whose cultures are in the main line of Near Eastern tradition. They have done so because of a conviction that the techniques and insights developed through the study of primitive societies are useful for the description and analysis of all societies. Although some anthropologists have ventured into the study of groups in urban centers, the majority of those interested in learning the ways of life of the co-heirs of their own civilization have concentrated on what have been called "folk" or "peasant" societies, or, to phrase it more descriptively, the rural populations of modern nations. Application of anthropological techniques to such groups has raised some new problems in method and interpretation.

The customary discussion of these new problems includes questions concerning the appropriateness of delineating a small rural village as the unit for observation when, as in Latin America and in Europe, such villages may not be economically, socially, politically, or culturally isolated from the larger societies of which they are a part. Awareness of this problem has led to special emphasis on the analysis of types of association between the territorially based group which is the main focus of the study, and similar neighboring communities, towns, and cities, and also on the analysis of the way in which national economic, religious, educational, and political institutions impinge on the life of the small unit. Such information and discussion are inherent parts of this study.

Another significant question is the extent to which the village chosen can be considered typical either of similar neighboring communities or of the culture of the entire nation, or of both. When national cultures cover large areas of varied terrain and have huge populations distributed in villages, towns, and cities, it is likely that there will be some regional and community variation in culture and social structure. It is therefore sensible to ask whether in describing the ways of life in the Greek village of Vasilika one also succeeds in describing the essential culture of other farm settlements and the values and attitudes of all Greeks now living in Greece. When we give lectures on Vasilika either to professional or to lay groups, someone always asks, "How did you choose your village?"

Anthropologists have concerned themselves with the methods of choosing communities for study in such a way as to guarantee some degree of representativeness. One solution to the problem has been to compare certain features of the village with the numerical and percentage distribution of those features in the nation as a whole. One might compare the age and sex distribution of the village population with that of the entire nation, or the age at marriage, or the size of families, or the proportion of farmers to shepherds, or the average real income, and the like, and conclude that if the village resembled the nation in these respects, it had some claim to representativeness.

Another solution, the one used in this study, is to choose a settlement which seems from my reading, my observation, and my discussion with Greeks to have frequently recurring features of rural villages, even if such features are not necessarily characteristic of all such settlements. One hopes that intensive study of such a community will be a contribution to the understanding of rural culture and social structure in the nation, and that some values and attitudes of the people observed will be shared by the total population. The discovery of which of the values and attitudes are shared and the more general question of typicality can be postponed until similar studies are done of rural communities in different regions and of town and urban populations of different occupations and social positions (cf. Sanders 1962).

We chose Vasilika in Boeotia for special study both because it exhibits some of the features just mentioned, and also because it is suitable for the application of anthropological field work techniques. Its common Greek plains village features include the compact arrangement of its houses, with the fields surrounding them, its accessibility to paved roads, its mixed subsistence and cash crop farming, and the existence within the village of a school, two coffeehouses and stores, several church structures, and a resident priest. In a negative sense, one of Vasilika's features is that there is nothing unusual in its history or present situation which would markedly differentiate it from other farming villages of the region. It has never been the subject of any special agricultural extension campaigns, none of the villagers have wealthy overseas relatives interested in improving the village as a whole, and it is outside the orbit of the tourist. If there is anything unusual about the village, it was the arrival of several shepherd families in 1950 and their subsequent political and social integration into the community.

Vasilika is suitable from the standpoint of field work techniques for several reasons. First, since it has a population of only 216, two field workers could expect to know everyone in the community. Second, the speech of the inhabitants is a form of Greek with only minor dialectic variations from the Athenian demotic form (see glossary) that we had studied in preparation for our work. And third, one of the families in the village was willing to have us live in the upper story of their house, which is located close to the center of the village.

Vasilika's way of life must be understood as completely representative only of itself, but in some of its general features it has most in common with other farming villages on the Boeotian plain. The degree to which the habits, values, and attitudes of the villagers resemble those of other Greeks, at this stage of our knowledge, must remain on the level of impressions. As a rural settlement, however, Vasilika has many features in common with farming villages that are segments of old national cultures in other parts of the world. The culture of the village is assuredly not in all its aspects a uniquely Greek phenomenon. Students of similar villages in other parts of Europe, the Near East, Latin America, and Asia will find many features of the culture and social structure of Vasilika familiar to them. But even these specialists will find a goodly number of features and especially of combinations of features that are entirely unfamiliar, for they are features that are uniquely Hellenic.

Two problems of particular relevance to anthropological studies of the rural populations of modern nations have been considered: the usefulness of choosing a rural settlement as the unit of observation, together with the new lines of investigation such a choice requires; and the selection of a particular settlement for study. These problems present their difficulties, but anthropologists working in old national cultures have some advantages; they can consult the works of other specialists. In Greece, for example, an anthropologist need not act as his own historian, economist, political scientist, psychologist, and sociologist. Folklorists have long been collecting oral literature and folk costumes from all sections of the country. Greeks and non-Greeks alike have produced many varied reports on Greek life and culture, both ancient and modern. Neither does an anthropologist working in Greece have to act as a geographer or agronomist—these specialties already exist and their practitioners can be consulted. Nor does the anthropologist have to discover the structure of the language for himself, nor is his vocabulary limited to what he can learn directly from the people he studies. An anthropologist working in old national cultures is able to concentrate his energies in the field on that aspect of his profession for which he is specifically trained and best fitted: the observation of the behavior of those he lives with for the purpose of discovering its regularities, its range of variation, its internal interrelationships, and its association or articulation with the culture of the nation of which the village community is a part.

There are, however, some unexpected mental hazards in doing anthropological field work in a society whose culture is a contemporary variation on one's own basic tradition. We had two opposite reactions to the way of life of the village; one was a strong sense of its familiarity, and the other was a surprised awareness of its strangeness. The sense of familarity grows out of the similarity of so many cultural elements with those one knows from home; the sense of strangeness partially from the often slight variation in the form of the elements, but more particularly from the way the elements are combined, from the new patterns created by a different organization of the items and by the different contexts in which they appear.

A trivial example may illustrate the point. If the cultural element under discussion is adult footwear, we are immediately conscious of familiar elements. Shoes and slippers are purchased, not manufactured by each family; men and women do not wear the same types; the man's shoe is a standard low oxford tie, and the women wear leather pumps with medium high heels, or cloth slippers. The shoes, pumps, and slippers are within the range of styles for such items available in the United States. But the contexts in which the Greek villagers wear their shoes and slippers provide surprises. Men in Vasilika wear ordinary oxfords for work in the fields, for walking in mud, rain, and even snow during the winter—with no other foot protection. When the fields are flooded for irrigation, men remove their shoes and work barefoot. Within their houses, men do not change into slippers; they do not own any. Women, on the other hand, wear cloth slippers both indoors and outdoors, around the house and in the fields, in all weathers and in all seasons. Their leather pumps are saved for church, for holidays, and for journeys. On such occasions women wear pumps regardless of the weather. They daintily pick their way through muddy, unpaved village paths and stand for hours in unsubstantial pumps on the stone floor of the unheated church each Sunday throughout the cold, rainy winter.

Ways in which the same cultural elements are differently combined in the Greek village from the way they are in the United States will be noticed as family organization, values, and the like are discussed. The hazard this kind of situation creates for the anthropological field worker is that he may not even become aware of certain characteristics of village culture because their superficial familiarity leads him to take them for granted. For example, once I learned that farm animals and stores of farm produce were not kept in the houses, I assumed they must be maintained in buildings of distinctive design. Although this turned out to be partially true, it was not entirely so, and many of the stone structures I had labeled as homes, because they had the same form as houses, were actually stables and storehouses.

The material presented in this book has been selected and organized in such a way as to emphasize the major interests and preoccupations of the villagers, rather than to demonstrate explicitly the ways in which knowledge about the village can be helpful for the solution of general anthropological problems of theoretical import. I am using the data on which this brief ethnography is based in connection with such problems elsewhere.

A final note is in order. In describing the people of Vasilika I have avoided using the term "peasant" for two reasons. First, the layman's concept of the peasant often includes the traits of stupidity and stubborn resistance to change that are by no means characteristic of the people of Vasilika. And second, social scientists have not yet arrived at a definition of the term that is generally accepted among them. References to the current discussion of this latter problem appear in the reading list.

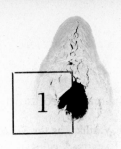

1

The Village. As a Setting

T HE VILLAGE OF VASILIKA lies almost at the foot of Mt. Parnassos on the Boeotian plain. The oldest of its fifty-odd houses were built in the late nineteenth century by the grandfathers of some of the now adult villagers. Most of them came from the village of Parori two miles to the northeast. Until 1933, when Vasilika sued for and won separate status, the two settlements were classified by the central government as one community (*kinotis*). The parent village still has the larger population, with some 700 inhabitants, while Vasilika, in 1955–1956, had 216.

Both Vasilika and Parori have come to be called by these names only since 1955. During the Turkish occupation, and for more than a century after the liberation of the region, the Boeotian villages used the names the Turks had assigned to them. Parori was Biskeni Aghas; Vasilika was Kravasaras. But in the last decade, patriotic considerations have led to a change from the old names to ones based on Greek roots. *Parori,* in Greek, means "near a mountain" and is an appropriate name for a village which rests in the foothills of Parnassos. *Vasilika* means "royal" and was the name of a hill in the region where a famous battle against the Turks was fought. In some cases, the names by which the villages were known in classical Greek times were restored. Drachmani, for example, once again became Elatia.

Most of the villagers of Vasilika, in 1961, still called the village "Kravasaras." Indeed, the new sign pointing to the dirt road which leads into the settlement reads *Kravasaras,* in spite of the designation of the village in the provincial records as *Vasilika.* This type of double nomenclature is common in the entire region. The wives of Vasilika, most of whom come from the surrounding Boeotian villages, frequently refer to their former houses by their older Turkish names. These are the names which evoke for them the emotions associated with "my village." Their husbands, on the other hand, often refer to their wives' home villages by the newly given names. An outsider must resign himself to learning the double nomenclature if he is to avoid utter confusion.

7

The Area Surrounding Vasilika

The inhabitants of Vasilika, as the village will henceforth be called, are farmers and shepherds. The farmers cultivate the land in the plains adjacent to the low-lying ridge on which most of the houses are built. As a consequence of the dowry and inheritance system in the region, some of the fields near Vasilika are owned by farm families in neighboring villages, and the Vasilika farmers own some lands in other sections of the Boeotian plain and even in the surrounding foothills. By and large, however, the inhabitants cultivate lands of the quality characteristic of the Boeotian plains. These lie in East Central Greece, north and west of the smaller plains of Attica. The flat land of Boeotia is one of Greece's few regions of moist, fertile soil. The Kiphisus river once flowed through the whole area, but earth movements and the porous limestone of the region, which permits underground drainage, have broken the continuity of the river's flow. The upper stream flows through a narrow mountain-bordered valley and then into a wide plain which was once covered by Lake Copais. The river is silt-laden, and the underground channels through which the water escapes tend to get blocked up. The land can not always absorb the waters of the winter rainy season as rapidly as they accumulate. Thus an especially wet winter can flood the fields so badly that they do not drain off in time for spring planting (Newbigin 1949:333). A system of controlling the waters exists for the land reclaimed by draining Lake Copais. However, the cultivated fields of Vasilika lie some miles past this region, and although the Kiphisus flows through their fields, the farmers have no method of draining off excess water. Consequently, they watch the winter rains with some apprehension. On the other hand, the regular winter flooding in ordinary years, along with the accumulation of alluvium enriched by humus, makes the soil suitable for two crops of wheat annually and for summer crops such as cotton and tobacco (Newbigin 1949:333).

Since the growing season for these last two crops is a dry one, the cotton always requires irrigation and the tobacco sometimes does. The natural underground drainage system makes it possible to drill good wells almost anywhere in the fields, from which water may be drawn by diesel irrigation pumps. Many such wells have been dug and are serving Vasilika's farmers. Within the village itself there are nine wells in regular use. Only an unusually dry year brings any danger of serious water shortage for either ordinary household purposes or for irrigation. The mulberry trees which line the main village street and the occasional trees which appear here and there among the houses flourish because of the good water table and, in spring and summer, provide a pleasing contrast of dark green to the predominantly brown and orange tones of the village's land and houses.

The people of Vasilika, like those on the other plains of Greece, not only have the advantage of larger tracts of more fertile soil but also are considerably less isolated than the inhabitants of the mountain villages. As will be seen, the easy access to roads and transportation to and from the village has important consequences for its culture and social structure.

The Boeotian plain is bounded by mountain systems and the sea. Running west and north, the Parnis, Kithaeron, and Helicon ranges as well as Parnassos itself separate it from the plains of Attica. The town of Lamia on the small Sperchios plain to the north and the west can be reached only by traversing parts of the Kallidromon and Ghiona mountains. To the east, an extension of the Kallidromon range makes access to the Gulf of Atalanti difficult. But the most important road which runs over and around the mountains and through the plains from Athens to Thessalonika has been paved throughout its length since World War II. It is now a two-lane asphalt highway which serves as a truck and bus route of major importance in the communications system of the country. In most of Boeotia, the highway runs more or less parallel with and not far from the tracks of the Athens-to-Thessalonika railroad.

The village of Vasilika lies on the slope of a low ridge just a half mile off this main highway. Since the summer of 1956, a local bus comes through the main street of the village twice a day, at 6:00 in the morning and at noon.

Going in the direction of Athens, ninety miles distant, the bus passes a British Petroleum (BP) station and restaurant a mile and a half down the road and traverses several villages. Its destination, however, is usually Levadhia, fifteen miles from Vasilika. Levadhia is the provincial capital and marketing center of some 12,000 population. Here bus connections to Athens may be made.

In the opposite direction, the nearest village of some size and importance is Kifisokhori. It lies five miles up the road from Vasilika. Kifisokhori has, among other facilities not available in Vasilika, flour mills, large grocery stores, barbers, doctors, a pharmacy, a movie, and several taxis. Whether they use the bus or load their horses with flour for the mill and walk by way of the shortcut through the fields, the people of Vasilika go most frequently to Kifisokhori.

Further north and off to the west, but only about eight miles past Kifisokhori, is Amphiklia. This town is the seat for tax collections and other governmental financial matters for the fiscal district in which Vasilika is situated. On the 16th of each month, for example, the priests of the village within Amphiklia's jurisdiction gather in the town to collect government salaries. Amphiklia also has a coeducational gymnasium (the approximate equivalent of an American high school and junior college combined). Several boys and girls from Vasilika live in that town to attend the school.

The people of Vasilika can also travel in the direction of the sea. The dirt road which starts at the highway leads to the houses of the village, then becomes the main street, and finally extends beyond the settlement between the borders of the fields and the foot of the ridge on which the village is situated. Never free of ruts, of dust, and in the winter, of mud, the road narrows and deteriorates further as it passes the last village house. Nevertheless, pedestrians, donkeys, horses, tractors, and even, with some difficulty, trucks and buses can get through. Half a mile past the last village house, at the banks of the Kiphisus, this road meets the road to Atalanti. Buses from Levadhia that have turned off onto the Atalanti road at the BP station will stop here if there are any passengers.

The asphalt and dirt roads are not the only routes by which the village can be approached. The local railroad station of Helikon is just a mile up the highway going toward Kifisokhori. Trains from Athens stop at Helikon at least once a day. The train can also be used to reach Kifisokhori. Thus, a resident of Vasilika can reach any of the main towns of eastern Greece with relative ease and at no great expense, even from the standpoint of his own standard of living.

The same transportation routes which enable the villagers to leave their homes also enable people and products to enter the village. Itinerant vendors of fresh fish, oranges, tomatoes, ice cream, cloth, crockery, sacred pictures, and the like reach Vasilika over these roads. Tinsmiths, blacksmiths, and cobblers use them to come to set up shop for a day or two near one of the coffee houses. The same roads bring gypsies who occasionally pass through the village to beg and to entertain. On the many occasions when family gatherings are in order, the town relatives of the villagers can reach Vasilika with ease.

This description has so far primarily concerned itself with Vasilika's accessibility to town or city centers of commerce, government, and recreation. But there are also paths through the fields and into and over the surrounding hills that lead to the neighboring villages. One can still walk or ride a horse or a donkey to reach these settlements. For the women of Vasilika, these are the important routes. By following them, they can reach the homes of their parents and their daughters, attend the engagements, weddings, and saint's day celebrations in their home villages, and perhaps help out when a daughter has a child. These same paths bring the relatives of Vasilika's women into the village on similar occasions. From the standpoint of the rural economy, this network of paths permits the movement of farm laborers among the villages. Indeed, it is in this way that the postman walks from village to village carrying the mail.

The stress on the many avenues of contact with other people and communities available to Vasilika's population should not lead one to imagine a bustling, busy center with a constant ebb and flow of traffic. The exact nature of movement in and around the village can be better understood if the spatial arrangement of Vasilika's buildings is known. Social relations among the villagers are also affected by these arrangements.

Inside Vasilika

The ridge, on the lowest slopes of which most of the structures are built, lies, as I have said, a half mile from the main highway and somewhat parallel to it. The highway runs from northwest to southeast, Vasilika's ridge from northwest to east. To reach the first village structure, one walks north about three-tenths of a mile on a dirt road leading from the highway. Vineyards and fields are on the right; to the left stands the new one-room schoolhouse built in 1959, with its play yard and surrounding wire fence. A stand of young pines and another of young cypresses, newly planted by the school children, adjoined the schoolhouse in 1961. On the road, past the schoolhouse, a little further to the west but on the same side of the road is Vasilika's cemetery. It is a small square area outlined by tall cypresses standing just inside the low stone wall which encloses the graves and the small church of St. Nicholas. Mass is said in this church in celebration of the birthday of its patron saint on December 6th. Sunday afternoon Easter services and funeral ceremonies are also held there.

Past the cemetery the road turns east, runs through the village, and constitutes its main street. Almost all the buildings of Vasilika are ranged for about one-fifth of a mile on both sides of this dirt road. Most of the houses are on the ridge side of the road; a single row of structures lines the field side. As one continues east on the village street and looks to the right on the field side of the road, he first sees fields and then the old school building. The next structure is the main church of the village, the church of St. Athanasius. It is the largest building in the settlement, and, like most of the others, it is constructed of field stone. Regular Sunday masses, Christmas and Easter services, baptisms, weddings, as well as the majority of saint's day and other special liturgies are conducted here by the village priest. The bell in the campanile of St. Athanasius summons the villagers to church, the children to school, and the men to an impromptu public meeting on the rare occasions when one is called to discuss village affairs. And, inevitably, the tolling of the bell announces the death of one of the villagers.

Separated from St. Athanasius by a very narrow alley stands a one-room structure which serves as the office for the village government. It now has a telephone, the only one in the village. Near the village headquarters and still on the field side of the road lives the owner of a combined store and coffeehouse. A ground-floor room of his house contains merchandise such as matches, cigarettes, lemons, salt, sugar, canned vegetables and fish, aspirin and penicillin, thread, and miscellaneous small items, while the outside space in front of the store is reserved for chairs and tables. From this coffeehouse, on the field side of the village, the rest of the structures are homes and their outbuildings, roughly in a line near the road.

Starting now at the western end of the village, and looking east at the ridge side of the road, one sees houses and their outbuildings occupying the lower third of the ridge. The uppermost group of homes were, in 1955, reed huts in which some of the shepherd families lived. Other reed huts served as storage houses. By 1961, the dwelling-huts had all been replaced by new brick houses, already wired for electricity but otherwise in various stages of completion. On the ridge side of the road the only buildings which are not exclusively used as residences are, first, another combined store and coffeehouse, which stands on the street diagonally opposite the first and is also a room in the house of its owner, and second, a nearly completed stone reservoir.

Finally, some two hundred feet past the last house and slightly up the slope, stands the small church of St. Cosmas and St. Damian, the patron saints of the village. Here the village celebrates its *paniyiri,* its patron saints' day festival, on the first of July. Mass is celebrated in the morning, and villagers from the surrounding countryside fill the small edifice to overflowing. Occasionally, other masses are said at this church in the course of the year. Except for the church of St. Cosmas and St. Damian, therefore, Vasilika's public buildings and its two commercial establishments are concentrated toward the end of the village that is closest to the turnoff from the highway.

The part of the village street which is between the two coffeehouses is called the *aghora* (market place), and it is here that the public life of the village is carried on. The bus stops at the *aghora*. Most of the itinerant peddlers stand there and loudly shout their wares. Government officials sit in one or the other of the coffeehouses to conduct business with the villagers. At the end of a day's work in the fields and throughout much of every day in the winter, Vasilika's men sit in the coffeehouses to talk, occasionally to play cards, and, incidentally, to drink coffee or, in the summer, soft drinks. On feast days and holidays musicians come to the *aghora*, and the villagers, their guests, and people from the neighboring settlements gather to listen to the music, and to take turns at dancing and at watching the dancers. For the most part, however, the world of the *aghora*, and, indeed, the public world of the village, is a male world penetrated sporadically by children of both sexes. Business with government officials or with artisans is conducted by the men. Men do the marketing from the peddlers of fresh foods, and buy whatever items are needed from the village stores. Little girls up to the age of twelve or fourteen, alone or with their brothers, may be sent to the *aghora* on errands, but older girls and women will venture into the area only to pass through it on their way to church or to the fields. I have seen a young mother from the eastern end of the village, when she heard the calls of a tomato vendor, walk to the edge of the *aghora* area. She stood some two hundred feet from the tomato wagon, shouted to the peddler to ask what his prices were, and then waited in the same spot until she could send a passing child to buy her tomatoes for her.

The private world of the villagers, which is more significant than the public one both from their own point of view and from that of the outside observer of the culture and social structure of the region, is concentrated in and around the homes. With a few exceptions to be noted later, each of Vasilika's married men owns the house in which he lives with his wife and children. The structural type and size of the houses and the arrangement of each family's compound of buildings varies partly with the age of the buildings and partly with the income level of the owners. The large older houses are two-story rectangular stone buildings with an outside staircase leading to the terrace of the second story. There is no way of reaching the upper rooms from the inside of the house. The terrace, with wooden plank flooring if there has been no recent renovation, and of cement, if there has been, is a constant feature of the two-story houses. The roofs are peaked and covered with red tiles. Stones are used to keep loose tiles in place. Large two-story houses built since the end of World War II are constructed on the same pattern, but with flat terrazzo roofs. Most of these are still constructed of the local stone. A second type of older house is smaller in area, has only one floor, and is built either of the prevailing stone or of whitewashed stucco covering a brick frame. Some of these structures have no windows, and when this is the case, they are more frequently than not used as combined storage houses and barns. However, several of Vasilika's families live in such windowless houses. There are also newer versions of the one-story house now being built in the village. They are one-room structures with red brick walls, flat roofs, and no facing of any kind to finish them off. This is the type of house several of the shepherd families have had built for themselves. They find them a considerable improvement over the reed huts. Two young farmers who have married girls from the village have also built houses like these for themselves in order to avoid having to live in the already cramped quarters of their parents.

The other types of construction in the village are stone-walled ovens which are usually extensions of the lower part of the house (access to them is always from outdoors), brick housing for the turkish-style latrines used in the village, stone parapets for the wells which are scattered throughout the village, and the occasional stone wall which surrounds a house compound. The most desired pattern for a household's compound in Vasilika is a large two-story house with an oven, one or two storage houses, a latrine, and a large yard with some mulberry trees, a grape arbor, and a small garden, all surrounded by a ten- or twelve-foot wall with one or two gates as the only mode of entrance and exit. One man in the village has just such a compound. Several others have similar ones, but with lower surrounding walls. For the rest, there may be fewer buildings and no enclosure, or perhaps the requisite buildings with a wire fencing as a substitute for the walls.

The first principle of arrangement of Vasilika's buildings is that places of public resort face the main street and are fairly close to each other at the western end of the village. The principle governing the arrangement of houses is different. They are individually oriented with respect to the street and to Mt. Parnassos (which is off to the northwest) but not with respect to each other. That is to say, the entrance to each house faces either in the direction of the street or directly away from the mountain. This is not true of outbuildings, however, the entrances of which are found on any of the four sides of the buildings. This combination of orientations and the habit of building enclosing stone walls or wire fencing, with the gates or paths through these on different sides, results in a clustering of structures randomly arranged with respect to each other. The single rocky path leading from one house door may reach the entrance of another house, or it may lead along a roundabout path which skirts the back of a storage house, or it may lead to a well yard or to a stone wall. A walk around several house compounds may be necessary to get from one house to the doorway of another which is right next to it. Some buildings have very narrow alleys between them; others are separated from each other by paths of differing widths and open spaces of varying size. The houses of Vasilika are not, therefore, arranged in neat rows with straight paths between, nor are they laid out in an orderly system of concentric semicircles or similar patterns of rectangles or squares. Since the buildings are of different heights themselves and stand on different levels of the hill and since there are no clear rows of paths, one does not get a panoramic view of the activities of the villagers as they move around close to their houses even when one looks down from the windows or verandas of the houses higher up on the slope. Instead, one may see only the back of another house, or a small part of a path which a neighbor uses. Even the houses directly on the village street are fairly close to it, so that the protrusion of one wall obscures the view from the roadside entrance of the next house. Four of the substantial village households along the main street have high enclosing walls on the street side.

Either by inadvertence or by design, such an orientation of buildings has certain consequences. It successfully limits the ability of the members of any village household to see directly just what is happening in more than two or three neighboring households. Except for such immediate neighbors, people may have to make a deliberate effort to find out what is going on in other sections of the village. And the signs may not be easy to interpret. The smoke rising from an oven down the hill indicates that the oven is in use. But it may be the owner who is using it, or some other woman who may have borrowed it to bake her bread. Or perhaps she is baking a *pita* (a kind of pie). Who knows? Besides, much of the movement of people to and from their homes has to do with what, from the villagers' point of view, are family affairs. Trips connected with the possible sale of tobacco, with the purchase of finery for a festival, with the preliminaries involved in arranging marriages, or with the supervision of any property owned elsewhere, are considered private family business. One therefore does not make a public show of setting out to attend to such affairs. People will make all preparations inside the house and leave just in time to catch a bus. If most people are indoors or in the fields that day, a departure may not be noted until the evening discussions in the coffeehouse. Or perhaps not even then, since few men follow a regular pattern of coffeehouse attendance.

The point here is not that the people of Vasilika cannot and do not learn about the activities of the other villagers, but that the acquisition of such information comes with some conscious effort and often with some difficulty. Once obtained it is highly prized. One gets the impression that about some matters, at least, everyone is playing a perpetual game of hide and seek. Each family does its best to keep certain aspects of its own affairs from leaking out and every other family does its best to uncover the secrets. Each group succeeds somewhat in its purpose and the taste even of limited accomplishment serves to keep the game going. The placement and character of the buildings in Vasilika contribute to the intriguing quality of the process.

Movement in and through the Village

To return to the general question of the pattern of traffic and movement in Vasilika: The public focus of the village is at the western end of the settlement, and remains on the level plain. Many visitors to the village, therefore, never travel further, either out east or up the hill, than the *aghora*. But some trucks, tractors, horses, mules, donkeys, wagons, and even occasional taxis are driven through the entire settlement on their way to and from the fields near the river. The villagers themselves contribute much of this kind of traffic in the spring, summer, and early fall when they go daily to the fields and transport equipment and produce on their animals or, as two families do, on tractors. They are joined by farmers from neighboring villages whose fields lie adjacent to Vasilika and who travel through the village to reach them. Trucks come to pick up cotton, tobacco, wheat for the mill, and the like and, therefore, are seen more frequently whenever the various crops are being harvested. In any case, whenever there is movement along the entire length of the settlement, it occurs most densely in the early morning just after dawn and in the early evening just before sundown. At these two periods of the day, in addition to the other traffic, someone from each of the households in which sheep and goats are owned leads the animals up the hill to the shepherds who will watch over them during the day. In the evening, the sheep are brought back again, but the goats often find their way home without any help. A first encounter with a lone goat coming around the corner of a village house, as it suddenly appears in the violet light of early dusk, is a startling experience. The soft light at the beginning and the end of these days is associated with the delicate tinkle of the sheep and goat bells as the animals move around the village. The entire ebb and flow of movement diminishes to an irregular trickle during the Mediterranean winter months from November to January when people stay in the village proper for most of the day.

Vasilika's shepherds and their families also participate in the main patterns of movement, except that the shepherds continue to go out daily through the winter and may leave the village entirely for the summer months.

But traffic in Vasilika is rarely a mass movement. Rather, there is always a range of time within which the villagers consider it feasible to carry out any activity. Each family moves at its own pace within the range. Even during the busy agricultural seasons, watching from the vantage point of a terrace facing a part of the main street at the east side of the *aghora,* one sees, first, a man going by in the direction of the river, leading a horse which carries a cultivator in its saddle; for ten minutes no one goes by, then a young man passes in the same direction; for five minutes nothing, then a woman and her grown daughter go past in the other direction carrying hoes for work in the cotton fields. A few minutes later, two young brothers go by, one leading and the other riding a horse sidesaddle; and so it goes until there is a longer period with virtually no movement at all. What is more, each day, even in the same season, the people involved in the movement will vary. The man who was first to go out one morning may leave a half-hour later the next; a girl who did the washing at home one day, and so did not appear at all, will be seen going out to the fields on the following morning. Such variation in activities both as regards the time when each of the village families starts on any project, and also with respect to the timing of activities from day to day by the members of any one household, appears again in the seasonal shifts of activities. The first major agricultural task in early spring is the pruning of the grape vines. For a period of several weeks almost every man who passes by is carrying a pruning hook. But here too, families start and end their pruning on different days. Only the comments on the situation are uniform. Each man complains of his blistered hands and aching back, remarks that pruning is especially hard work because it is the first job in spring after the winter's rest, and usually finishes by saying, "What can we do? Wine is good, but it takes hard work."

The movement of people in and out of Vasilika is not dependent on the agricultural cycle alone. I have already mentioned the visits of vendors, traders, and government officials to the village. Each saint's day brings some visitors to Vasilika, for the men and boys of the village celebrate the birthday of the saint after whom they were named, and not their own birthdays. On St. George's Day, for example, relatives who live in surrounding villages come to visit the George in Vasilika who is kin to them. The number of the visitors on these days is thus directly related to the number of men and boys in the village who have been baptized with the name of the saint being honored. On St. John's Day, St. George's Day, and St. Constantine's Day, for example, there are many visitors to Vasilika. There is no one named Spiros or Petros in the village, so that St. Spiridon's Day and St. Peter's Day bring no visitors at all.

The periods of greatest density of population in the village are the two or three days of *paniyiri* (the patron saints' day festival), when relatives and strangers by the hundreds come to the village for the festivities, and Christmas and Easter, when those who formerly lived in Vasilika return to their *patridha* for a few days. Vasilika is least fully populated in midsummer when individuals and families attend the *paniyiria* of other villages in the region. They usually choose those villages in which they have relatives, and stay for a few days. At this season, also, some families go to watering places for a week or two, or camp on Parnassos to avoid the heat of Vasilika.

The arhythmic quality of the movement of people, animals, and vehicles through the village has been described. It now remains to say that the pace of movement is always slow even when it is most purposeful. No one strides briskly along the road or paths of the village; only children are ever seen running. The pace seems to be set by the slow walk of a loaded horse or mule or donkey. The villagers take the long leisurely strides they need to accompany these pack animals, whenever they go from place to place, even when they walk without them. Slow action is characteristic also of the performance of any task. No one is ever in a hurry. Women cook and serve with efficiency but without speed; men load a horse equally efficiently but again without speed. Their movements are controlled, and the exercise of that control gives an impression of vitality, of a tenseness which makes the slowness a sign of power and deliberation, never of lassitude or indifference.

When a visitor returns to Vasilika, he may ask, *"Ti nea?"* "What's new?" He often receives the quasi-rhyming response *"Isichia,"* "All quiet." The response means "The round of life is going on as usual. Besides, nothing much ever happens in this place, anyway." And in some sense, the villagers actually believe what they say. The village is the physical center of the lives of the inhabitants; in spite of their trips out of it, and the coming of visitors to the village, the people of Vasilika see and talk to their fellow villagers more frequently than they see and talk to nonvillagers. They even express considerable satisfaction with some of the obvious village-wide changes of the last few years such as electrification and the provision of a reservoir for water to be piped to the houses. But the village is neither the moral center of the life of the villagers, nor is it, as an entity in its own right, one of their dominant interests.

Starting an ethnography with a chapter called "The Setting" is a common practice among anthropological writers. By implication, what will follow is a kind of play for which the "setting" provides the scene. Such a beginning is particularly appropriate to Vasilika, because the village has, for its inhabitants, as well as for the observer, some of the quality of a stage-set. The people of Vasilika seem to think of their fellow villagers as acting the role of the chorus in ancient Greek drama (it is the chorus which comments on the action). The main action of the "play" in the village lies in the life of the family. We have heard villagers exclaim in connection with some intense family situation, "*Ti dhrama!*" "What a tragedy!"

From an anthropological point of view, the family in Vasilika is significant not only as the focus of interest for the villagers, but also as a separable unit of the social structure of the settlement. In cultural terms, the patterns in which families participate as a unit form a large part of the culture of the entire community. The next three chapters are therefore devoted to the activities of the village families.

2

The Family: Economic Activities

THE STRUCTURE AND ACTIVITIES of the family as the most significant social unit in Vasilika will become clearer in the ensuing discussions. For the present, the family in the village may be defined as what has variously been called the "elementary," "nuclear," or "conjugal" family; that is, a husband and wife and their children. It is the welfare of his own family as a corporate entity which motivates the actions of the villager; and the family is the group whose members work in cooperation to try to maintain or to improve their common position. The villagers measure prestige and honor by the degree to which a family succeeds in fulfilling its obligations. From their point of view, the essential family obligation is to maintain a ratio between property and children such as to enable each child, when the property is divided in equal shares among all the children, to maintain, in turn, a decent standard of living for his family. This goal commonly requires not only an effort to conserve the wealth received from previous generations, but also, if possible, to increase it. The villagers act as if they conceive of the family as a kin group which conserves, accumulates, and transmits wealth from one generation to the next. The ability to transmit wealth is especially important. The villagers consider a man who is rich in lands but has no children an object of pity; the man's wife is considered even more unfortunate. This is because the contemplation of the success of their children gives the life of a married couple a large part of its meaning. In the operation of the inheritance and dowry systems in the region, a son may be given his share of the patrimony in the form of an education and a daughter given hers as her dowry at marriage. An educated son who has a civil service job in a town, or a daughter whose dowry was large enough for her parents to have found a schoolteacher husband for her, can give to the parents lasting inner satisfaction and the joy of being able to tell of their child's exploits. To be able to sit and watch such adult children, or even an industrious farming son, as they talk to visitors of their adventures, or as, on a feast day, they eat the food their parents have carefully prepared for them, is a form of pleasure so well recognized that there is a specific verb to express it: *kamarono*.

The economic activities of the family through which its members actually carry out a large part of their obligations are usually conducted by an entire household. A household in Vasilika, however, is neither limited to nor does it always include a husband and wife and their children, that is, a family. This is a result of the operation of the marriage, dowry, and inheritance system in the region (to be discussed fully in Chapter 4), and of unpredictable specific circumstances. Here it is sufficient to say that in 1961, of Vasilika's fifty-one households, twenty-six were composed of the elementary family; eight, in addition to the parents and their children, included the widowed mother of the husband; seven had a husband and a wife living alone; and three included one married son and his wife and children living in the same house with his father and mother and unmarried brothers and sisters. Of the remaining seven households, each had its own unique composition because of recent deaths in the family or other special circumstances. Whatever the particular situation, however, no Vasilika household includes anyone who is not a kinsman, nor indeed any adults outside the kinship range of parents, their grown children, or adult brothers and sisters.

Of the fifty-one households in Vasilika, thirty-five are headed by farmers who own some land. Although, for various reasons, these farmers are not all equally dependent on their land holdings for their total subsistence and income, their round of life as independent working farmers is one important expression of the aims and obligations of their families. The yearly round of agricultural activities is devoted principally to the production of grapes for wine, wheat for bread, and cotton and tobacco for cash. The farming households also engage in subsidiary activities which contribute to the production and processing of the main crops, and which add to the food supply and income of the households.

Major Crops

The first event of the agricultural year is the pruning of the grape vines. Since grapes are not a commercial crop, each farmer devotes only one or two *stremata* (four *stremata* equal one acre) to viticulture. Wine is made and consumed at home, and each farmer aims to produce only enough grapes to keep him in wine for a year. Pruning of the grape vines starts after the winter rains have abated and the early spring sun appears. Only two or three "eyes" are left on a vine, and the cuttings are carried back to the storehouses to be saved for use as fuel for spit-barbecuing the Easter lambs. Again, as we have seen, farmers are particularly conscious of fatigue in the course of the three or four days it usually takes to do the pruning. Palms have softened over the winter, the wooden handle of the pruning hook raises blisters, and the unaccustomed stooping and pulling motions cause backaches. After the pruning, deep hoeing is done to pile the earth around the short, stout vines. The work is done with a long-handled heavy hoe and, in Vasilika, is considered man's work, as is the pruning. Since the two jobs in the vineyards must be finished quickly so that the men of the household may turn to plowing cotton fields, those farmers who prefer to start plowing earlier, or who have larger vineyards than the household can handle alone, sometimes hire labor for the hoeing. Sons who are not needed on their father's land may work for others in the village or may go for several days to work for relatives living in neighboring villages. In either case, they are paid a daily wage of between forty and sixty drachmas (thirty drachmas equal one dollar) and get their board as well. It requires three man-days of labor to hoe one *strema* of vineyard. Hiring labor for this is considered expensive. Farmers with fewer land resources may, in order to avoid the extra expense, ask their wives to do some hoeing. Although such a procedure is frowned on in Vasilika, a farmer considers the practical necessities of his situation as more important than any possible loss of prestige. Moreover, village opinion itself recognizes the force of a man's practical needs, and tempers criticism to the nature of the specific circumstances. This phenomenon is characteristic of Vasilika and will be mentioned again.

The vines continue to need some attention from time to time until the grapes have ripened. Wine-making begins in September with the gathering of the grapes. September itself used to be called *triyitis* (the time of the grape harvest). It is an occasion much enjoyed, since men, women, and children all pick the grapes together, talk and joke as they do so, and eat a little of the produce besides. Four or five people can pick the yield of the two *stremata* in a few hours. The pack animals carry baskets of grapes back to the house. After making certain that there are no leaves among the fruit, the men of the household wash their feet and then trample the grapes. The must collects in shallow basins and is transferred to barrels. A sample of must from each barrel (the usual household's yield is two barrels) is taken to a chemist in town to check whether sugar or alcohol or both may be needed. Payment for this service is made according to the weight of the wine the farmer will treat as a result of the chemist's advice. Besides adding the recommended quantities of sugar and white alcohol to the must, the farmers also add enough resin to make up two percent of the contents of the barrels. Resin is sold by vendors who circulate among the villages in trucks during the wine-making season. The resin gives the wine of the Greek countryside its name, *retsina,* and its characteristic flavor. In classical times the ancient Greeks and later the Romans added resin to the must as a wine preservative. It still has this function, but to the present villagers, as to the ancients, the resinated wine has a pleasing taste and, in Vasilika, is much preferred to nonresinated wines. We once started to serve a bottled Greek nonresinated wine in our village home but we were quickly informed by our village guests that it was poor indeed, and one of our visitors left the table to go home to bring a carafe of his own superior wine. Those to whom drinking a mild form of turpentine seems unpalatable at first can develop, as we discovered, a taste for *retsina* and come to enjoy it very much.

Wheat fields are plowed and sown in the fall, in late October and early November. A farmer can plow his wheat fields with a horse or two pulling a steel plow, or he can hire a tractor to do the job. The hiring of the tractor includes fuel and the services of a tractor operator.

Two farmers in Vasilika own tractors—one made the purchase in 1952 (a British Ferguson), the other in 1956 (a British Fordson). They were bought on the installment plan with credit extended by the Agricultural Bank of Greece. The tractor operators are a son and a nephew, respectively, of each of the owners. Both of the farmers who purchased tractors have landholdings which are large for the region, perhaps as many as sixty *stremata* but divided into tracts of some ten to twenty *stremata* each. Even if the land were not divided into such small parcels, there would not be enough return on so little land for economically sound use of a tractor. Both the bank management and the farmers are well aware of this, so that credit for the purchase of the machinery is given with the understanding that the owner will use the tractor as a capital investment and earn income from it by renting it out.

Farmers decide to hire or not to hire a tractor for the fall plowing on the basis of practical considerations of the moment. If weather conditions have been normal in the late summer and early fall, a farmer will be more likely to proceed with his horse-drawn plowing. If, however, early rains have delayed the cotton picking and all hands are needed in the cotton fields when the wheat fields should be plowed, a farmer may hire a tractor to be sure that the job gets done before the winter rains. Most of the farmers maintain a horse to use as a pack animal, in any case, so that it is obviously cheaper to plow with the horse. For increased efficiency, two farmers sometimes contribute one horse apiece, so that the team of horses working on each of their fields in turn will get the work done faster and at no additional cost. For wheat, the farmers say, the deeper plowing of the tractor is not important, so whenever possible they work with the animals. For cotton, as we shall see later, they believe tractor plowing increases the yield. Generally speaking, as one might expect, the farmers with fewer land resources tend to make less use of the tractors than those who can expect a good cash income from their fields and so can afford the outlay for the hire of a tractor.

After the broadcast sowing of the wheat (which is done on each *strema* immediately after it has been plowed) and the dragging of the fields, what remains is some light hoeing to be done in February and March, the spreading by hand of some chemical fertilizer at about the same time, and when the weather warms up, the spraying of a chemical weed killer by means of a hand-operated pressure pump. A farmer who does not own such a pump borrows one from a neighbor, and no charge is made for its use.

Harvesting of the wheat crop is done almost entirely by machine in Vasilika. Reaper and thresher combines, with their operators, make the rounds of the Boeotian plains villages at harvest time in June. The threshed wheat is weighed out in the fields and the machine operators are paid promptly with twelve percent of the crop. Chaff and straw left in the fields are collected by the household and made into small packages to be used for bedding down the animals. Each farmer may set aside four or five *stremata* of his wheat field to be reaped by hand with a standard sickle. He then hires a thresher with operator at a cost of eight percent of the amount of the wheat threshed. This machine leaves the straw in suitable condition for a baler which is hired next to press the straw into bales for food for the horses, mules, and donkeys.

The harvesting machinery is privately owned by entrepreneurs in the towns. Simple threshers have been known and used on the Boeotian plain for a generation at least. The combine has appeared only since World War II and the hay baler only since the early 1950's. What accounts for the increasing willingness of the farmers to pay for machine operations on their wheat crop? Unquestionably, the growing efficiency of cotton production and the success of cotton and tobacco as cash crops enable the farmers to concentrate their labor and attention on cotton and tobacco production and to let the growing cash value of the crops make up for the loss of a certain percentage of the wheat crop. However, chemical fertilizers and weed killers have increased the wheat yields, and since payment for machine harvesting is in kind and not in cash, the entire transaction can be managed at what to the farmers is a minimal cost.

A household uses its own wheat for making its bread, and bread is still literally the staff of life, the basic food for the people of the village. Wheat is also used for a kind of cereal called *trakhana* and for egg noodles. It is given as payment to the shepherds, whose wives turn the wheat income into their families' bread supply. It continues to be used as an alternative medium of exchange for fish, olive oil, olives, coffee, and other household necessities not locally produced. As we have seen, the wheat straw is useful for the care of animals, and finally, in an emergency, some wheat can always be sold for cash.

A typical farmer of Vasilika reserves four or five *stremata* of his land for oats, barley, and clover. These furnish food for the pack animals not only during the winter, but also in the early summer when the animals are permitted to graze in the oat and clover fields as the crops mature. A small corner of a grain field may be used for lentils and beans, which add to the household's food supply.

The crops which most interest the farmers of Vasilika today are cotton and tobacco. Because of the dry summers in Boeotia cotton production in the region depends on irrigation. The high water-table makes well-pump irrigation feasible. This system is also suited to the patterns of the rural social structure since it requires no centralized control or authority—each farmer household can dig its own well and work its own pump for its own fields. Any man who has not yet purchased a pump can hire the use of one owned by a farmer with adjacent fields.

Cotton became a significant cash crop for Vasilika around 1936 when one of the farmers who had heard about horse-driven well-pumps set one up for himself and the other farmers soon followed suit. Since World War II, British-manufactured diesel pumps bought on the installment plan with credit extended from the Agricultural Bank have replaced the horse-drawn equipment. Diesel pumps, like the tractors, may be rented by the day and the renter pays for fuel also. The market for the use of the pump goes beyond the village itself since farmers in neighboring villages whose cotton fields lie adjacent to those of Vasilika's pump owners often want to hire the pumps. Here again, the rent income helps to defray the cost of the machinery.

Work is begun in the cotton fields shortly after the winter rains abate in February or March. Like the wheat fields, the cotton fields are sometimes plowed with horses. But, apart from the two farmers who own tractors, a number of farmers believe that the increased yield from the deeper plowing a tractor furnishes is more than worth the cost of renting the machines. Planting is ordinarily done by hand, but in 1956, a few farmers owned machine planters, and several farmers were borrowing them to try them out for the first time. The utilitarian and essentially nontraditional attitude to farming characteristic of Vasilika's inhabitants is illustrated by what one of the farmers had to say about using a machine planter."I've planted half of my forty *stremata* of cotton by hand and the other half by machine to see which will turn out better. It's an experiment, you see." The machine planter must have been better, because in 1961 the same farmer had planted all his cotton by machine.

A few rows of maize are planted in the midst of the cotton fields to provide feed for chickens. Boys and young men like to roast and eat a few ears of corn out in the fields in late August, but corn is not considered proper food for human beings, and eating corn bread is believed to be a sign of dire poverty.

Once the cotton starts to grow, in late May and June, the hoeing begins. This is arduous labor which includes weeding, chopping up the weeds, and arranging the chopped weeds around the cotton plants as a mulch. Hoeing is done by the girls and women of the household, although men sometimes help. If a farmer has as many as twenty *stremata* planted to cotton, it is at this point that he may begin to use hired labor. Generally, the women of the village who are not busy in their own cotton fields are called upon first. These are the wives and daughters of the shepherds and the wives and daughters of the few farmers who have small enough land holdings so that their women have time left over after hoeing their own fields. When these supplies of excess labor are exhausted, farmers turn to relatives and non-kin in the neighboring villages.

The hired women who came from other settlements used to live in the house of the farmer who employed them, and used to be fed by him as well. In 1961, however, the farmers were reporting a system they much preferred—the use of tractors and trucks to bring women from the neighboring villages in the early morning and to take them home again in the evening. This obviated the necessity of housing and feeding four or five girls at a time during several different periods in the course of the cotton growing season (cotton is weeded and hand cultivated at least twice and sometimes three or four times during the season). The women of Vasilika's households were especially pleased at the change, because although they enjoyed having the company of the hired women, who danced and sang in the evenings, they very much disliked the additional work involved in housing them. After a long day in the fields, the farmers' wives and daughters had to prepare a hot evening meal for the work crew and, before dawn each morning they had to pack the bread, cheese, and olives which would provide a morning collation and a midday meal in the fields. The decrease in food costs, in work, and in the inconvenience of having strangers in one's house, were considered, in Vasilika, well worth the increase in daily wage from about forty drachmas in the 1950's to the 1961 wage of approximately sixty.

Even with the release from housing hired labor, the period of cotton cultivation is the most difficult of the year for the people of Vasilika. The weather is hot and often humid as well. Much of the hoeing must be done directly under the hot sun with the hoer bending from the waist to manipulate the short-handled hoes. To protect themselves from the sun and from being scratched by the plants, both the men and women keep their arms and legs covered and shade their faces. The women wear long lisle stockings, their oldest long-sleeved flannel or cotton dresses with high necks, and kerchiefs which they draw around to cover the lower half of their faces. Men and women alike are embarrassed when outsiders see them in their old, worn, earth-spattered field clothes. "See us!" they say as one walks by the fields during this season of the year, "in our rags. What can we do?"

In spite of the weariness and inevitable backaches cotton hoeing brings in its wake, the women must still continue with the ordinary housekeeping chores. Once every week or so, they get up at two or three o'clock in the morning to sift the flour and knead the dough for bread; an occasional day free from hoeing gives them time to do the accumulated family washing and ironing; and each day brings its own complement of bed-making, sweeping, cooking, and dish washing. Although the men have more frequent respites from hard physical work in May and June, both men and women obviously lose all the weight they gained during the less active winter months.

Irrigation, which begins in July, is a man's job. The cotton fields are irrigated twice or three times in the course of the summer, and a farmer and his son can ordinarily manage all the work. If not, the women of the household often help, or the farmer can hire men. But finding male farm labor is more difficult than finding women. Young men, when they reach twenty-one, serve for two years in the Armed Forces, and if a young man is not regularly needed on his father's farm, or has been educated, he is likely to have left the village for a town. Nevertheless, sons of poorer families, whether they attend gymnasium during the winter or not, are available for summer farm labor from the time they are thirteen or fourteen years old.

The task of irrigation consists of clearing shallow ditches into which the water will be channelled, and then channelling the pumped water into them. Men work barefoot and sometimes stand in water up to their knees. Occasionally they work through the night with torches for light, and one gets the impression that the men and boys enjoy such nights for the sense of adventure they give. The need to walk around in the mud and the inevitable spattering of the mud over their clothes and their faces are what the men find disagreeable about irrigation, and once again, they complain of their unsightly appearance.

In October and November, if the weather has been normal, the cotton is picked. This requires a prolonged period of work by many hands, since the plants mature at different times: some cotton is ready for picking each day for a period of at least two months. Women are again hired to do the job. But this time, the women from Vasilika and from the neighboring villages who had been free to do the hoeing are not necessarily free to spend away from home the prolonged period required for picking. The local women can and do hire out when they are free, but they can be free only sporadically, for their own fields also need some attention every day, even if their cotton production is not extensive. Therefore, the intermittent wage labor of the neighborhood women is augmented by labor from more distant regions where no cotton is grown, and where the early fall is therefore a slack season in the agricultural cycle. In 1955, six Vasilika farmers took the train to Trikala (near Larissa) and brought back with them thirty women who then worked in Vasilika for almost two months. Each of the farmers took responsibility for five or six women; he paid their round trip fare, put them up in his home, and furnished them with food. As a net wage, he paid them for picking the cotton in his fields one to two drachmas per *oka* (one *oka* equals two and eight-tenths pounds) of cotton picked. A serious, mature worker can regularly pick about forty *okadhes* a day.

In the picking season the farmer's main concern is to finish the job before the winter rains set in. If prolonged rains come early, the value of the cotton is lowered, and the processing of it involves additional expense. If the cotton has to be picked while it is still damp, it must be picked with the pod, and later must be separated from the pod by hand. The farmers paid hired workers a drachma per *oka* for the job.

While the women are picking cotton, the men of the household weigh the filled bags, keep records of the amount each woman picks, and use the horses, donkeys, or mules to haul the cotton from the fields. It is stored in the stone barns, in the lower storage rooms of the houses, and, as a matter of fact, when other space is no longer available, in any room in the house. Trucks from the cotton gins in Levadhia come through the village and collect the cotton. Farmers keep track of the weight of cotton they send to be ginned but do not identify their own sacks. The ginning costs six percent of the original weight of the cotton, a percentage which the gin owner keeps for himself. The farmers use the seed returned to them for the next year's planting, and also have some of it pressed into cakes for use as supplementary fodder for the ewes at lambing time. The cotton itself is again stored in sacks to await sale to merchants who visit the villages. During the season, the cotton is also used as a medium of exchange. Itinerant vendors selling fish or oranges, for example, are willing to take raw cotton instead of cash in payment.

The price at which the farmers sell the cotton to the merchants is never high enough to satisfy the farmers, who feel they get a disproportionately small share of the ultimate value of the cotton. We were once host to some urban visitors and to some of the village's leading men. In the course of the afternoon a heated and eloquent discussion on cotton prices developed. The farmers contended that by the time they paid the costs for machinery, fuel, hired labor, and calculated, in addition, the value of the labor of the members of their households, they made scarcely any profit at all on the cotton. The visitors, on the other hand, insisted that it was wrong to include the labor of their households as part of the cost because for the women, in particular, work on the farm was a way of life. "After all, what else would they do?" the visitors contended.

The discussion was extraordinarily illuminating because of the clarity with which it defined the villagers' overt conception of their own purpose in farming. The Vasilika men were thinking of their farms as commercial enterprises and were applying to their operation, however unwittingly, modern cost accounting principles whereby the labor of members of a family is a proper charge against profits in a family enterprise. The Vasilika farmers do not actually keep sets of books on their farming operations, but they do keep records, in an unsystematic way, of some transactions. Even though they do not keep exact accounts, they think of their agricultural activity as a business enterprise and evaluate the success or failure of their family farms in monetary terms. The visitors, in contrast, were recommending that Vasilika's farmers think of themselves as peasants, not as entrepreneurs. In other words, the visitors were suggesting that farming in the Boeotian countryside is a way of life. They meant that its satisfactions should come as much from the means as from the ends. For the women, at least, the visitors contended, work in the fields and in the subsidiary agricultural tasks was as good a way to pass the time as any other and that their work was merely one aspect of their roles as wives and daughters. The farmers said, in effect, that their women were performing specialized agricultural tasks primarily as a means to an end, the end of earning a profit from the operation of the family farm. Therefore, contended the farmers, when women do agricultural jobs, they are properly considered as agricultural labor, like the hired workers with which the households ordinarily supplement their manpower.

The villagers' arguments were entirely consistent with their behavior. To accept machinery and chemical aids which increase yields and save time, as Vasilika's farmers have done, presumes that they place a value both on quantity of production and also on man-hours of work. In other words, they run their farms, at least partly, from the standpoint of rational economic efficiency. Actual accomplishment of efficiency is far from complete in Vasilika. Our point here has to do with attitudes and tendencies.

The tobacco crop gives an even greater cash yield than cotton in relation to the investment, and its cycle of production fits well into otherwise slack periods. Vasilika's farmers would prefer to raise more tobacco, but the acreage devoted to this plant is centrally controlled by the Greek government. Each year, farmers are assigned the right to plant a specific number of *stremata* to tobacco, with the variations dependent on the anticipated world market for the crop.

Men plow tobacco fields in November at about the same time and in the same way as they do the wheat fields. In December, the men prepare the frames for the tobacco seed beds, and the women plant and tend the seeds. The seed beds are usually near the farmer's house. During this month, the canes which will later be used for hanging the tobacco are cut and stored. The villagers use burlap lightly stretched over reed frames to protect the seedlings from the cold and rain. After the winter rains, the women keep watering the tiny plants and fertilize them regularly. The chemical fertilizer which is provided by the Agricultural Bank requires careful handling. Women explain that too much fertilizer will burn the tender plants, and they take pride in their success in applying just the right amount. Conversely, they ridicule any unfortunate woman who is so unskillful as to have burned her plants. As the tobacco plants grow and the weather gets warmer, occasional rains make worms and snails a hazard in the seed bed. In March and April, at dusk, women are seen stooping at the seed beds collecting and killing these parasites.

The winter of 1955–1956 was an unusually cold and long one, and Vasilika still had some snow in March. Many households had to plant tobacco three or four times in the course of the winter and spring, and several households ran out of seed. The abnormal weather with flooding rains in March and no rain for much of April delayed transplanting. Ordinarily, the tobacco plants are about four inches high in early April, and can be transplanted then. By that time, the fields are usually sufficiently well drained and yet still have enough moisture for the tobacco to "catch" as the villagers put it. In the spring of 1956, the fields were too dry by the time the tobacco was ready for transplanting. Some households resorted to carrying water from the wells, a gallon can at a time, making a hole with a small steel hook, pouring a small amount of water into the hole, and then placing the young tobacco plant into it. Everyone was thoroughly disgusted with the back-breaking and tedious labor, not normally connected with the tobacco crop, and men and women alike (both work at transplanting) were vociferous in their complaints. Tobacco, here, needs no irrigation. Therefore, although some of the farmers were willing to put their pumps into operation to irrigate the tobacco fields during this extraordinarily dry season, most of the tobacco fields were too far from the irrigation wells to make that entirely feasible.

Usually in late June or early July, the outer leaves of the tobacco are ready to be picked. Both men and women work at plucking the three or four outer leaves of the plants, and then sit in family groups on the ground in the shade stringing the leaves in preparation for hanging them over the canes. This kind of work normally follows the hoeing of cotton and is especially welcome. As we would pass from one part of the village to another, at this time, we would hear exclamations of satisfaction and enjoyment as people explained what a relief it was to be able to work out of the hot sun, near their houses, and sitting down besides. The tobacco stringing is a job in which even very young children can help, and they sit with the adults piercing with holes the tobacco leaves through which their elders eventually pass the string. Throughout the summer, periods of cotton hoeing alternate with periods of tobacco cutting and stringing.

Once strung, the tobacco is hung up to dry on frames which are set up on poles out of doors. A tobacco growers' association has recently distributed canvas shelters to prevent the soaking of the leaves by unexpected summer rains. When no such canvas is available, the tobacco is taken inside the barns each night. In October, the dried tobacco is pressed into bales by machines the farmers have for the purpose, and is then ready for sale.

A farmer can get 720 *okadhes* of tobacco from 6 *stremata* of land, and if he succeeds in selling the entire crop at 30 drachmas an *oka*, he receives the equivalent of $720. This is a very good income, indeed, especially when it is added to that derived from cotton.

Vasilika farmers are obviously in need of some capitalization to finance what have become considerable investments necessary for producing their wheat, cotton, and tobacco. Whether or not the farmers' savings would be adequate to finance their crops, the fact is that Vasilika farmers do not want to use their accumulated savings to invest in their own farms. Cash drachma savings are exchanged for gold English sovereigns or French or Italian specie, which accumulations are then set aside for the dowries of the girls of the family or to pay for the education of a son. The only notable exception to this use of savings is that the farmer who becomes wealthy enough to feel that his obligations to his children are taken care of may buy land if the opportunity presents itself. At the same time that the farmer does not want to spend savings on the current production of his crops, he is eager for an increased cash income to secure the future of his children. Increased cash income is possible only through investment in his farm. How does he get out of the dilemma? He willingly accepts credit from the Agricultural Bank of Greece. In addition, farmers accept from the bank the needed seed, artificial fertilizers, and chemical weed killers and insect sprays. March is the month in which the loans are made by the bank, so that the farmers always receive their money before Easter. Both the manager of the Agricultural Bank in Levadhia and we were aware of the fact that some of the money was used for Easter finery and Easter feasting. We had the impression that the farmers considered the loan as cash income to be spent as they wished. The repayments of principle and interest due in October were viewed by the farmers as something like an additional expense or tax chargeable against current income from the produce, and in this sense, not as expenditure of savings.

Miscellaneous Crops

Each household maintains a small kitchen garden near the cotton fields. This location permits the farmers to irrigate and to tend to the garden at the same time they work with the cotton. Both men and women work in the gardens to raise tomatoes, eggplant, cucumbers, squash, and melons of various kinds, but only to the extent necessary for immediate consumption by the household and its hired farm labor through the growing season. No effort is made to produce surplus for canning or for any other kind of home processing. Besides the summer vegetable gardens, in the early spring, the women of a few households fence off a rectangular area near the houses and plant spring onions, lettuce, spinach, and a type of lima bean called *kukya*. The wire or reed fencing keeps out both animal and human thieves. These small plots are not carefully tended and their produce is consumed in a few weeks.

Some mention of the most important vegetable food for the villagers may be included: the wild greens (*khorta*) that grow at the edges of the fields and on the hillside. Collecting the greens, which entails finding, recognizing, and cutting them close to the ground with a small knife, is another task of the women and young girls. Some greens are available all year round and children can collect them when the women are busy. However, on occasion, even men and boys will gather a few on their way home from the fields. *Khorta* are not served every day by any means, but they are a fairly common article of diet.

Some fruit trees are cultivated on the village lands. One farmer has as many as ten apricot trees in his cotton fields, but most have a cherry tree or two in the vineyard, perhaps several fig and peach trees in the wheat fields, and an occasional pear, quince, pomegranate, and mulberry tree on some other holdings. The fruits are eaten as they ripen, except that the women prepare from some of them the sweet preserves which are a necessary adjunct of village hospitality. Homemade *gliko kutalyu* (sweet jam) usually lasts through to midwinter, but after that, the villagers buy what they need.

Home canning or other food preservation, therefore, is not a significant addition to the annual locally produced food supply in Vasilika. Even the recognized need for more fruit preserves has not impelled the women to try to convince their husbands to increase the size of orchards. Tomato paste is an important condiment in village cooking, but again, the farming households buy the commercially canned paste, and the women do not prepare any themselves, although, as we have seen, they raise some tomatoes.

Government agricultural extension agents made an effort in 1954 to convince the young girls to can pears and plums as part of a competition. The government recommended fruit canning to the rural women for several reasons: to improve the winter diet without additional cost, and to encourage the increased cultivation of fruit trees as one means of improving drainage on the land. But there has been no increase in canning or in fruit production, and by 1959, even the prize certificates, which had been displayed on a wall of the *saloni* of the house in 1955 and had drawn our attention to the campaign, had disappeared. When asked, the farmers say they could not adequately guard so many trees and the ripe fruit might be stolen. "Why should our family raise fruit for others to eat?" they said. They shrug their shoulders at the soil drainage argument.

The effect of planting fruit trees is, of course, not immediately visible, nor could an eventual improvement in drainage, if it did occur, be an obvious demonstration of the efficacy of orchards, for the cause-and-effect relationships between the two might be obscured, for the farmers, by all the other variables which affect drainage. The reluctance to embark on long-range improvements which are backed by abstract scientific knowledge not directly observable in the farmer's own experience is in direct contrast to his willingness to try short-range experiments the results of which are easily and immediately demonstrable. Indeed, in 1955, the school teacher was criticized for having the school children help in the care of fruit trees that the provincial government had arranged to plant on the highway near the village.

The farmers are willing to try some variations if they can use the techniques they know and understand. Cotton prices had been low in 1958. In 1959, therefore, about four or five of Vasilika's farmers planted some of their cotton lands as melon patches, intending to sell the produce in Levadhia or in Athens. By 1961, they had gone back to raising cotton, because the experiment had failed. One of Vasilika's farmers prefers to use his irrigated land as a truck farm, and he and his son sell the produce in the surrounding villages. He argues that with a vegetable crop the cash returns are faster and he incurs fewer debts.

Livestock

Each of the farm-owning households also maintains some animals. One or two horses, a mule or a donkey, some five to twenty sheep, and one or two goats constitute the range of livestock ownership for each household. The horses, as we have seen, pull the plow and the cultivators in the fields. Together with the mules and donkeys, they also serve as pack animals. The pack saddle of wood and leather is of a design that has remained virtually unchanged from Homeric times. It is used not only for carrying loads, but also for carrying people who ride sidesaddle among the paths, through the fields, and between the villages. Sidesaddle is the normal riding position for both men and women, but in the spring, when the horses are let out to pasture on the hillside, the young men of the village sometimes ride them home bareback, astride, galloping and whooping in what they call *kaouboi* fashion.

The villagers do not give their animals individual names, and they take no particular care to keep them physically comfortable. They will hitch them in the shade of a tree in the fields if that is possible, but the farmers may not remove the saddles for an entire day. The animals are beaten with switches and kicked to make them work, and children are permitted to tease donkeys. Nevertheless, the villagers occasionally pat one of their beasts and sometimes encourage children to kiss the ears of a horse and to feed it a lump of sugar.

Sheep, except for the lambs, are cared for by the shepherds. Of a hardy mountain breed capable of surviving the rigors of Greek pasturage and climate, the sheep as milk and wool producers augment the food supply and sometimes the cash of the farmers. Sheep milk is rarely drunk in liquid form, but yoghurt and cheese are prepared from it. The white cheese is a staple of the villagers' diet. They eat yoghurt less frequently and prepare it only as a special dish in milk season.

The villagers raise a special lamb each year to slaughter at Easter, but otherwise rarely eat lamb or mutton. They will consume a sheep that dies of age or disease, and they slaughter sheep for some special occasion such as a wedding, or someone's name day. At shearing time, wool is boiled in large kettles, washed in the river, sent to town for carding, and then dyed and spun into thread at home by the women. In each household the women weave the rugs that are a necessary part of a girl's trousseau with wool from their own sheep—at least as long as it lasts.

Goats are raised for their meat and, in households with young children, for their milk. Adults rarely drink the liquid milk. As a form of pasteurization, the villagers always bring the milk to a boil before serving it, and the children drink the milk while it is still warm. In the more prosperous households, the women use both sheep's and goat's milk as an ingredient for a kind of milk and egg custard pie and for a sweet milk and rice dish served with sugar and cinnamon. But these foods are in a class of special treats and are served mostly in spring and early summer when the milk supply is at its height. Goat meat, however, is often a less elegant substitute for lamb on special occasions. Kids are raised for the Christmas feast, and the measure of the success of a household's participation in the village's *paniyiri* (patron saints' day festival) is expressed by the number of animals (goats and sheep) slaughtered for the feast. The more visitors to the house, the more enjoyable the day is felt to be; the more visitors, of course, the more meat is eaten. When asked whether the *paniyiri* had been successful this year, one farmer answered, "Oh yes; we slaughtered three!"

Chickens are also an additional source of food and sometimes of income for the villagers. Families keep about a dozen fowl. They roam the house yards, (there is an effort made to keep them off the village street, and all hands join in shooing them out of the houses), and roost at night in the stone stables or in the ground-floor storeroom of the houses. The villagers like eggs, and eat them in various ways, but their production is also, of course, seasonal. The chicken is most significant for the part it plays in Greek village hospitality. The villagers will say, "Come to our house for a proper meal (*trapezi*). We'll kill a chicken for you." And that is quite literally what they do. Occasionally enough chicks survive to create a surplus from the household's point of view. Such poultry is sold to buyers who come around from the nearby towns. Chickens are rarely considered an extra source of food for ordinary household consumption.

A watchdog is a common addition to a household's collection of farm animals. The people of Vasilika believe that thievery is a constant danger to be guarded against and prefer, if possible, not to leave their household compounds totally unguarded. Whenever possible, some member of the household stays around the property even if it means sacrificing a visit to a feast at a neighboring village. If all the members of a household are out working in the fields, a dog is left at home. Ordinarily, however, dogs are tied up all day and the farmer, just before he goes to sleep, frees the dog to stand vigil through the night. Dogs are trained to bark at any unusual noise or at the approach of any person who is not a member of the household. The villagers, especially the women, are very much afraid of the dogs and consequently avoid going out at night. On one occasion, when the women and girls of the village had sat together in the church until long after dark, they set out for home with groups of neighbors clustered together, holding on to each other, walking fast, and shuddering and exclaiming with fear at the clamor made by the dogs. It should be added that in actuality, there are few thieves in the village and that the dogs rarely bite anyone.

With few exceptions, dogs, like the other animals, are not considered pets. They are not given names and are referred to simply as "our dog." Parents permit young children to play roughly with them and to tease and abuse them as they wish. The animal is fed scraps of bread once a day, and there is a feeling that there may be some advantage to keeping it slightly hungry. The dogs also act as scavengers whenever horses or other large animals die in the vicinity of the village. Further evidence for the completely utilitarian attitude of the villagers toward their dogs is the diminution of the number of these animals in the village since the introduction in 1960 of electric lights on the street and paths of Vasilika.

Variations in Wealth

This chapter has dealt with the most important methods of providing subsistence and income in Vasilika from the standpoint of the typical small farm owner. However, all the farming households of Vasilika do not have land or other resources of equal value. Among the thirty-five land-owning households of Vasilika there are perhaps eight whose total holdings range from one to fifteen *stremata* and who own only a few sheep and goats. These households usually own donkeys, however, and occasionally, a mule and some chickens. Along with the four farm households in Vasilika who own no land whatever, these eight are the groups who must find wage labor in the village or in the neighboring communities. The level of living of both these groups is close to what is needed for bare subsistence, and a bad agricultural season leaves them close to destitution.

Another eight households are those of farmers whose land-holdings range from about fifteen to thirty *stremata* and who maintain themselves at what is considered an acceptable standard in the village, but who do so by a narrow margin. In several instances, these are households with children too young either to help in the farm work or to supplement income by wage labor.

Slightly more than half of the total number of farm-owning families— some nineteen—might be considered substantial farmers who may have better or worse years but whose present situation is reasonably secure. The largest land owner in the village has about 150 *stremata,* several men have something like 100, and the rest have holdings of 40 or 50 *stremata.* Forty *stremata* are regarded by common consent as a minimum for a decent standard of living for a farm household of four. Among these farmers, some own enough sheep to get additional income from selling surplus animals, but most have just enough sheep to supply milk, cheese, and meat for household needs. These farmers also have one or two horses.

A gross difference in the quantity of property owned is not the only factor effecting the income variation among the households of Vasilika. Soil fertility and drainage conditions are not the same on all the village lands, so some farmers get greater yields from smaller plots of well-situated fields. In addition, the members of several farm households get supplementary income from various sources besides wage labor. Bee-keeping, for example, is becoming an increasingly popular supplementary activity. Three households have as many as a dozen hives and sell the honey. A few households raise pigeons as an extra source of food, and now and then one or two may join together to raise a pig. One farmer's son has what might be called the "fish concession" in Vasilika. He contracts to buy the fresh fish from an itinerant vendor and then sells the fish in Vasilika at a tiny profit.

The proprietorship of the coffeehouses in Vasilika enables two of Vasilika's households substantially to supplement the income which they derive from their agricultural holdings.

Two young, still unmarried girls have had training as dressmakers. One of the girls, who learned her skill in Athens, spends all her time sewing and rarely contributes to fieldwork on the farm. The second girl, who had her apprenticeship in Levadhia, works on clothes for her customers in intervals between all her field and household chores. Every woman in the village can do some sewing and several have foot-driven machines, but the two seamstresses are kept busy and add to the cash income of their households.

The traditional role of the village priest is occupied in Vasilika by a substantial farmer, with a wife, five grown children, and several grandchildren. He not only performs his regular religious duties but is also the head of the church and the few properties owned by it. He receives a small salary from the state, and also derives income from performing baptisms, weddings, and funerals. Greek Orthodox tradition requires the priest to officiate at other occasions, such as the dedication of a new home or the termination of a woman's forty days of seclusion after childbirth, and he receives small money gifts for these services. But on the tax rolls of the community the priest's occupation is listed as farmer. This is a reasonable designation because both he and his wife, natives of the village, have inherited some local lands. The priest's household, therefore, participates in the agricultural cycle common to the rest of the farmers. Although the priest now confines himself largely to supervision, if there is an unexpected need for extra labor, he tucks up his flowing robes and pitches in.

The village church organization provides for three additional salaried posts: two farmers serve as chanters and an elderly widow as sexton. Finally, the formal political organization of the village includes the position of secretary to the village council. This office is a minor civil service post which requires no qualification other than literacy, pays a small monthly stipend, and is usually held by the appointee as long as he performs his duties satisfactorily.

In all the cases just described, the supplementary activities are superimposed on the grape-wheat-cotton-tobacco farming base. The shepherds of contemporary Vasilika, however, have a significantly different round of life which there is insufficient space to discuss fully here.

Specialization of Labor

Sheepherding as a specialty is relatively new to the village. Eight of Vasilika's ten shepherds and the members of their households are called *Vlachi* by the villagers. Most of these people come from Agrafa, in Euritania, in the northwestern part of the Greek mainland. Their fathers and grandfathers were shepherds, and the present group in Vasilika is the first generation ever to have settled anywhere with the intention and reasonable hope of staying. They augment the income from their own flocks by caring for those of the farmers as well.

From the point of view of the *Vlach* shepherd households headed by men (two are headed by widows), the settlement in Vasilika is a satisfactory change in their circumstances. In the years between 1950 and 1956, they had succeeded in building up their own flocks to the point where the sale of sheep, milk, and wool enabled them to have a small cash income to add to the money their women earned as hired agricultural labor. With a cash income, their diet no longer needed to be restricted largely to bread and cheese. The houses of the shepherds have improved since 1956. By 1961, all the shepherds' families were in houses instead of reed huts, and two of them were living in their own newly built one-room brick houses.

Perhaps most important to the shepherds' sense of well-being is that they have been admitted to citizenship in the *kinotis* of Vasilika, and that their children are receiving an education. The adult men had had to teach themselves and their children just enough reading and writing to be able to keep track of their commercial transactions through the year. Indeed, one shepherd, when asked what he thought about when he was out alone with his sheep, replied that he spent most of the time calculating how many sheep and how much milk to sell under the different possible price conditions of the coming season. What pleases the shepherds in Vasilika is that their children will have, as a result of a more formal education, some opportunities to follow a calling other than that of shepherd. In 1961, one of the shepherd's sons had already successfully completed a year at the gymnasium. Some of their daughters have married into the farm families of Vasilika, and even if these farmers are among the less prosperous in the village, such a marriage conveys prestige on the girl and her family in the eyes of the shepherd community.

Finally, the shepherds are grateful for the fact that several of them are settled in the same village and that it is possible for them sometimes to herd their flocks together. They are less lonely—they have company (*parea*)—and to have companions to talk to is considered a basic good by all the people of Vasilika.

In the first chapter, the movement of itinerant traders, vendors, artisans, and professionals into Vasilika was mentioned. The village has no resident carpenters, stonemasons, saddle-makers, barbers, tailors, or doctors; but the very existence of such specialists and the expectation that they will come from time to time, demonstrate an important characteristic of the household economy of

Vasilika's inhabitants and some of the congruent attitudes. The householders of Vasilika take it for granted that they will use part of their produce, in kind or in cash, to pay for the services of various specialists. They rarely make repairs on their houses or on their equipment; they rarely make shelves or simple pieces of furniture. In short, they do not have the habit of pottering and tinkering about the farms either from necessity or because they enjoy it. Vasilika's farmers and shepherds consider themselves specialists; they view themselves with pride as experts in farming and sheepherding, and assign the same dignity to the expertness of others. To say of a man, *"Kseri ti dhulya tu,"* "He knows his work," is a compliment, and the villagers use the phrase often. They do not expect a man to know how to do anyone else's work. One specialty is considered enough.

Such a point of view means that a farmer, if his saddle strap breaks, does without a saddle or borrows someone else's until the saddle-maker comes by, even if it means several weeks of inconvenience. In one of Vasilika's households, the stone wall of one side of an oven was accidentally broken by a tractor plow one day in April of 1956. At the end of July, the wall had still not been repaired —even temporarily—because the stonemason with whom the farmer was accustomed to deal had not yet had time to come to fix it. In the meantime, the women baked their bread in a neighbor's oven. We learned later that the entire oven was finally rebuilt in the spring of the next year.

When a farmer wants to cover his earth floor with cement, or when he wants the walls of his house whitewashed for Easter, he often pays to have these jobs done by a "master." On one occasion, a stonemason was persuaded to put screens on the windows of the house we lived in, but he went to a carpenter to have wooden frame pieces cut to the proper length. A final illustration indicates not only the existence of this point of view, but also the way in which those in Vasilika might greet a different one. The village house in which we lived had several broken windowpanes when we moved into it. Since the winter rains were due, we thought it imperative to get new glass in. My husband went to Levadhia, purchased glass and putty, and replaced the broken panes. The farmer who owned the house watched my husband work. He kept making the sign of the cross and repeated again and again in awed tones, "A professor who is also a master glazier!" The farmer himself had never thought of repairing his own windows, and for anyone in as exalted a position, from Vasilika's point of view, as that of "professor," to make such a repair had for the farmer a touch of the quality of a miracle.

With the increasing use of machinery on the farms, the villagers may be forced into learning mechanical skills; but the emerging pattern seems to be one in which the tractor operators and a village man who learned mechanics in the Greek Air Force have enough skill to make minor repairs and are called on by other farmers when they need help with their pumps. Major repairs must still await a mechanic from Levadhia. For the Vasilika farmers, however, the inconvenience of having to wait for expert personnel to repair machinery is not a source of special irritation. American farmers, who have been accustomed to acting as their own mechanics, are now beginning to deal with machinery so complex as to require expert repairs. Such dependence is new and annoying for them. But Vasilika's farmers easily fit the need for mechanics into their old patterns.

The constant utilization of specialists means that the farmers and shepherds of Vasilika have not for generations expected to be economically self-sufficient, but have always assumed that some part of their produce either had to be sold to buy services or had to be directly exchanged for them. The innovations since 1950, which have increased the proportion of cash crops raised, have involved no new concepts, nor have they required the development of any new attitudes. What has happened has been an extension and intensification of the already existing patterns. This is equally true of the purchase of foods as it is of skills. Olive oil, macaroni products, coffee, sugar, lemons, and dried fish have long been common articles of diet for the villagers and have never been produced in the area. Additional income has increased the consumption of these items and has made for somewhat greater varation in the diet, but the assumption that a considerable amount of food must be purchased is an old one.

Specialization in Vasilika has noneconomic consequences as well. Since a village farmer who has time to spare from his work in the fields and from his care of his draught animals does not spend it on repair and maintenance chores on his property, he has the time to go to the coffeehouse to sit and talk. In the late fall, one farmer kept saying, "A few more days of work, and then we will sit in the store. We sit all winter." Although he exaggerated the situation, his comments represented the regular expectation that for men, at least, relief from field chores was a relief from *all* kinds of work. The division of labor characteristic of the Boeotian countryside gives the men of Vasilika some true leisure time.

The foregoing discussion of specialization and division of labor in the Boeotian countryside should not leave an impression of a rigid set of expectations from which there are never any deviations. Although the pattern is a clear one, as in so many other aspects of the culture of Vasilika, individual variation, even to the point of reversing the ordinary expectation, is tolerated. For example, one farmer decided to construct a new oven for himself without the help of a stonemason or bricklayer. Everyone watched the progress of the small structure with interest but without any special comment. When, unfortunately, the entire structure collapsed just before it was finished, the men in the coffeehouse thought it a great joke and laughed heartily at the farmer's discomfiture. Only then did they remark on his lack of good sense in not getting an expert to do the job. He was not condemned for attempting to do something different; but he was ridiculed all the more strongly when he did not succeed. In less striking instances, farmers often assist an artisan with his work, and may even occasionally try their hands at whitewashing or laying a few bricks and the like. The point here however, is that it is neither a matter of pride nor of pleasure to have skills in many activities, and men and women alike prefer to avoid the chance of making themselves look ridiculous by trying to do something at which they are not certain to succeed.

Many of the economic patterns described in this and the previous chapter have become characteristic on the Boeotian plain only within the last twenty-five years, with considerable acceleration of change since 1950. Farmers in their fifties remember a childhood in which wheat was the major crop, with some corn, chick peas, and lentils as a supplement. Only a small amount of cotton was raised. Each household owned more sheep, horses, and mules than the present villagers. The animal dung fertilized the fields, some fields were permitted to lie fallow each year, and whatever cash income there was came from the sale of surplus wheat and small quantities of cotton, wool, and milk. The farmers all agree that one householder, working alone with occasional hired help, derives more income from his patrimony of 35 *stremata* than his father gained from 180 *stremata* worked with the help of several sons.

The increased mechanization on the farms of Vasilika and the more extended and intensive cultivation of cotton and tobacco have unquestionably increased the cash income of the villagers. The same conditions have led to increased indebtedness and a greater dependence on world markets.

Every household in Vasilika has accepted the new techniques and has been affected to a greater or lesser extent by the consequences. Whatever differences exist in methods of cultivation are dictated by the differences in immediate practical possibilities and necessities in each household, and there is no consistent pattern from this point of view which distinguishes one group of Vasilika households from another. From the standpoint of agricultural techniques, there is neither a progressive faction nor a conservative faction in Vasilika.

The uniformity of acceptance of change has been possible in Vasilika, I believe, because all the villagers, farmers and shepherds alike, work for the same goal: the enhancement of the honor and prestige of the family. One important culturally approved means of achieving the goal is the upward mobility of family members. But upward mobility rests partly, at least, on an improved material standard of living. Any change which enables a village family to increase its material wealth is, therefore, welcomed after a consciously empirical assessment of its effectiveness.

One of the methods by which a family can express its social position in Vasilika and its aspirations toward mobility is by the way it uses its income. The next chapter will discuss, therefore, some of the consumption habits of the villagers.

3

The Family: Consumption Habits

INCREASED INCOME resulting from technological advances in Vasilika has given the present generation in the village a wider choice of alternatives for alloting their resources than that enjoyed by their predecessors. The first call upon the family's income, after the needs of subsistence, is felt to be the accumulation of a dowry for the daughters and (since there is rarely land enough for all) the provision of an education or apprentice-training for all the sons except the one or two who could eventually be provided with enough land to farm profitably. The process by which these obligations are fulfilled is the subject of the next chapter. Here, our concern is with the goods and services used by the villagers, with particular emphasis on the overtones of meaning that accompany them.

The differences among the households of Vasilika in furnishings, foods, clothing, and hospitality patterns are not great on an absolute scale, but the small differences have, on the local scale, as much significance to the people of Vasilika as the corresponding differences do in any middle-class suburb in the United States. Family self-respect is maintained, and family rivalries are carried on in the village partly by demonstrating levels of taste through consumption habits.

What the villagers admire and try to emulate are standards of living and of taste as they perceive them to exist in the towns and cities. Their knowledge of these standards is acquired through the first-hand information brought back by their town relatives and by what they themselves notice on their own visits to urban centers.

The base to which the new standards are adapted, or for which they are substituted, is a set of patterns for rural living customary in the Boeotian country-side.

Inside Vasilika's Homes

Let us first consider the house. A new two-story house has the greatest prestige, but any family that builds a new house, even if it is only the small one-room brick house, gains some standing in the eyes of the villagers, although mild ridicule of the insignificant efforts of people of low prestige is not unknown in the village.

In the two-story houses, old or new, the ground floor typically consists of two rooms, one of which has cement flooring, with stuccoed walls and a fireplace. Many families use this room for all purposes: as kitchen, living room, and as the bedroom for all the members of the family. The women cook in the small fireplace, always conserving precious wood, the annual supply of which is usually purchased in October. They place two thin logs in the form of a V so that only the point at which the logs meet actually burns.

The only characteristic of the room which qualifies it as a kitchen is a wide window ledge, hollowed out to the depth of two inches, and lined with cement. The shallow basin slopes toward the window with a short length of metal tubing pushed through the outer wall of the house. A small water container with a spigot at the bottom is hung on a side wall above the shallow cement-lined basin, and the kitchen appointments are complete. Waste water drains through the tubing out into the yard of the house. The villagers often hang some towels near the basin and wash their hands and faces there each morning. The women of Vasilika used to agitate for the construction of a sink, both because it was a sign of progress and because it would ease some of their work. In 1961 they were eagerly awaiting the piping of water into the houses.

The lower floor all-purpose room is furnished with a few straight wooden chairs with cane seats, and may also have a table and a bed. Proper beds are not essential, however, because thin pallets can be brought out at night and placed on boards resting on wooden saw horses to create a bed, or may be merely laid out on the floor. The women pile the bedding, including folded pallets, sheets, and blankets, neatly in one corner of the room and cover the pile with a white rectangular cloth bedding-cover especially designed for the purpose.

The second lower room has an earthen floor and may be used for storing household supplies, wine-barrels, and agricultural produce. Among the less prosperous families, the lower floor may consist of only one earthen-floored room in which a curtain hanging near one end separates the living section from the storage area.

The upper story, apart from the terrace, may have several rooms with wooden plank floors and stucco walls. A second fireplace, sharing a flue with the lower one, may become the focus of what the villagers call the winter room. It is a smaller version of the all-purpose room below.

The remaining second-floor room is called the *saloni,* and is best designated in English as "the front parlor." It is the ceremonial room of the house, the part in which the family represents itself to the outside world. Visitors are ushered into the *saloni* and are expected to remain there. At name day celebrations, at the *paniyiri*, at Christmas, at engagement and wedding parties, guests are greeted in the *saloni* and may be served food there. Most of the time it is an uninhabited room, but because it represents the family to the world outside and because the patterns of hospitality in the village often require a family to entertain without advance notice, its furnishings are the best in the house and the room is always kept clean and in good order.

A typical *saloni* in Vasilika has a large square table placed in the center of the room. The table-top is covered with an ornamental cloth, often snowy white. A glass bowl commonly occupies the center of the table. It is often filled with slightly yellowed photographs of members of the family and relatives living away from the village, and with the most recently received postcards or greeting cards.

Virtually every *saloni* contains one or two large trousseau trunks placed along the wall. Their tops are usually covered with an ornamental white cloth. These trunks serve as storage places for bed linens, table linens, extra sheets, pillow cases, and table covers, which were part of the wife's trousseau. They also are repositories for the trousseau being prepared for the daughters of the house. No matter how low the income level of the family, there are always at least some token *rukha* (linens) as dowry. Again, regardless of income, every housewife serves her guests fruit preserves in small crystal dishes and the liqueur which accompanies the preserves in tiny crystal glasses, and proffers both items on a tray.

A *saloni* may contain no other furnishings, but often the one bedstead owned by the family remains there to be used only by guests. If the family owns a wardrobe they may display it in the *saloni* and store their best clothes in it.

Wedding photographs of the husband and wife of the household, and of their parents or their married children are hung on the walls of the *saloni*. Additional framed photographs of relatives who no longer live in the village also decorate the walls. Often a large framed mirror hangs on the same wall as the photographs.

Approximately ten of Vasilika's families had battery-operated table radios in the *saloni* in 1955. Since the electrification of the village, additional families have purchased radios on the installment plan. By 1961 it had become customary to turn on Greek folk music programs during the midday meal and in the evenings. Since 1958 several families have purchased elaborate chandelier-like fixtures, holding two or three electric bulbs. These are placed above the center table of the *saloni*.

The terrace of the two-story house has a variety of uses. Here the family may perform some simple household task. The women may hang their wash on wires stretched along the poles which support a sheltering roof. Here, too, they may set the table for the Easter feast. The entire family may sleep out on the terrace in the heat of summer. Whatever else the terrace is used for, however, its edge is always lined with plants of various kinds, potted in whitewashed gallon tin cans. Some are flowering plants, but many are herbs, especially basil, which the women use in cooking. The villagers, men and women alike, are passionately fond of flowers. In 1961 their comments of satisfaction about the impending innovation of piped water frequently included some mention of how they would be able to plant flower and herb gardens more profusely once the process of watering them became so much less tedious. They value plants and flowers both for their colors and for their scents. A sprig of fresh basil is a common offering to a guest, with the admonition, necessary only for non-Greeks, to rub a bit of it between the fingers to release its aroma. Indeed, the sense of smell is a far more frequently functioning mode of perception in Vasilika than in America. The villagers investigate unrecognized substances by smelling them, the quality and freshness of food is tested partly by smell, the decision as to when food is properly seasoned or as to when it is cooked sufficiently is partially determined in the same way. A more active use of the olefactory sense by the people of Vasilika, then, provides a source of information, of data to be interpreted, and also makes for added pleasure through the enjoyment of aromatic substances. The converse of this situation, however, is that the villagers are equally sensitive to what to them are unpleasant odors. For example, the odor of kerosene burners disturbs them greatly and they were reluctant to use such burners for cooking, and certainly for heating.

A little more than one-third of Vasilika's houses conform in all major respects to the type I have just described. These represent an ideal for the settlement to which those who do not yet have such houses can aspire. The people of the village have watched four families move into new houses of this type since 1950 and have seen several other families, since that time, renovate their old houses to conform. The aspirations are by no means unrealistic.

In the meantime, the other families in Vasilika live in houses of various types. A few live in the one-room stone houses with earth floors and no windows, in which animals occupy the corner of the room farthest from the entrance. Several live in the new one- or two-room brick houses. But the majority of the village's families dwell in one-story stone houses. Here, one plank-floored room is the *saloni*. There may be a second room serving as bedroom, and still a third, an earthen-floored room in which some cooking is done over an open fire. One end of this may also serve as a storage-room or stable. In these houses, the *saloni* has the same furnishings as in the others, but it is usually smaller and, since it is the only room with a fireplace, it serves also as the winter room of the house. It cannot be saved for guests or for special occasions.

Every house in Vasilika, regardless of the economic level of its inhabitants, has a corner of one room just under the ceiling set aside for religious objects. The central object is an icon of a saint of the Greek Orthodox Church. Often included are the framed wedding crowns of the married couples living in the house. A small lamp, arranged so that the light swings between the icon and the crowns, hangs from the ceiling.

The lamp was formerly lit by the wife or daughter of the household on the eve of every sabbath and of every feast day of the church. Since the advent of electricity, the small oil lamp has been replaced by a red electric light bulb which is kept lit at all times. This sacred corner is most frequently next to the bed that the husband and wife of the household use as their own.

The wedding crowns, white wreaths of small artificial flowers, are a necessary part of the Greek Orthodox wedding ritual, and, indeed, give a name to the ceremonial to distinguish it from an engagement. *"Stefanothikan akoma?"* "Have they been crowned yet?" is one way to ask whether a couple are married or still merely engaged. The crowns, which were blessed as part of the wedding, symbolize the founding of a new family under God, and their preservation is an expression of the desire to preserve the health and welfare of the family. That the intercession of the saints is a valuable form of assistance in coping with the problems of life is taken for granted in Vasilika; the icon with the light burning before it and the prayers addressed to the saint constitute a regular plea for the holy one's protection of the family.

The importance of the house as an adjunct of the life of the family is further emphasized by the request each family makes to have a priest bless a new home before the family moves in. An *ayazmos,* as it is called, places the house under God's protection, in the villagers' view, and the ceremonial is significant because building a house is a new and hazardous venture for a family whose success in this world as in the next, it is assumed, is ultimately in God's hands.

Cleanliness and Order

Sanitary facilities in Vasilika play a part in each family's striving for sophistication. A few households have no latrines. The majority have a small wooden outbuilding or a partitioned section of a storehouse for a Turkish-style toilet. This consists of a large excavation in the ground lined with stones and rocks, covered by wooden planks which form the floor of the latrine proper. There is no seat, but the planks are arranged so as to leave a small opening over which one squats to relieve himself. The newer facilities stand as separate structures made of brick, and the floor is cemented so that there is a slight slope toward the center opening. Finally, the best of these arrangements is one in which a specially designed ceramic floor fixture is imbedded in the cement flooring. From the villagers' point of view, the newer latrines are not valued because they constitute better sanitation, but because the villagers' urban relatives have been ridiculing them for not having some kind of toilet.

Just as the public world of the villagers is a world of men, so the house in Vasilika is primarily the domain of women. Women take pride in the skill with which they accomplish their many housekeeping tasks; they gain some satisfaction from completing each day's ordinary chores, as well as from the successful and skilled completion of their trousseau items. The standards of good housewifery in the village require considerable expenditure of time and energy on the maintenance of the home. Villagers value order and cleanliness—order in the sense of stylized neatness, and cleanliness as an avoidance of obvious dirt. We have already mentioned the neat piles of bedding covered with snow-white cloth. When the household has no wardrobe, there is a white covering over the clothes hanging on the wall that protects them from dust, and also creates an impression of a single unit instead of looking like a haphazard collection of garments. Kitchen utensils as well as farm equipment are kept in the storehouses or in the part of the lower floor used for storage. Thus village rooms, even the all-purpose ones, have a bare look. Since even kerosene burners are usually kept in storage places when they are not in use, the visible equipment in village rooms is not an accurate index of the family's utilitarian property. The use of the storage spaces, always hidden behind at least a curtain if not a door, has some of the quality of the well-known circus act in which a small army of midgets emerges from a tiny automobile. Carafes of wine, chunks of cheese, eggs, coffee, olives, rice, and coffee grinders, kerosene burners, flour, troughs for carrying bread, pots and pans, as well as farm produce and equipment such as cotton, tobacco, pruning shears, long needles for tobacco stringing, chemical fertilizer, and the like, appear when they are required as one or another member of the household disappears into the storage space and, after a short time, comes out with the necessary article. Only bread and recently purchased items are commonly visible in the village rooms. The loaves are placed on a high shelf and the women sometimes cover them with a cloth.

Orderliness in the village homes, then, is the result of a preference for keeping living space fairly free of equipment needed for household and farm chores, and, indeed, keeping this equipment hidden from view. The women spend considerable time and energy taking things out and putting them away, particularly because they make no special effort to provide a regular place for each item.

What the villagers do object to is, as we have seen, the dirt, the dust, and the mud that accompany so much farm work and that they try to keep away from themselves and from their good clothes and out of their houses. Cleanliness consists in keeping mantel-covers snowy white, in washing and pounding rugs once a year, in scrubbing wooden floors and staining them with a yellow dye before a feast day, in seeing to it that steps, terrace, outhouses, and, occasionally, the entire house are whitewashed before Easter, in having washed and ironed table cloths and napkins for guests, in wiping glassware just before glasses are used so that they will shine, and in wiping grease off the edge of a plate. Cleanliness does not consist in a concern for scientific sanitation; soiled aprons, for example, may be used as dishcloths. Once a cloth has dusted or polished or dried any article, and so removed all surface evidence of soil, the article is clean in terms of the villagers' concept of cleanliness. Such cleanliness, however, is regarded as essential for good housekeeping.

The women of Vasilika have no sense of urgency about accomplishing household tasks for the tasks' own sake. Although they ordinarily wash dishes from the previous night's meal, make beds, and sweep in the early morning, other tasks, including bread-baking, are put off until conditions are favorable and they choose to do the jobs. The chores do not rule the women; the women have control of the chores. The order in which they are done, and the particular time a woman decides to work at them, is up to her. It is the end result that matters.

Clothing

Apart from the house, its outbuildings, and furnishings, the most important item which signifies a family's degree of modernity in Vasilika is clothing. The old traditional rural costume of the region has not been worn in Vasilika, on the estimate of the oldest residents of the village, since their childhood in the 1890's and early 1900's. Couples were married in the old costumes somewhat later than that, but brides and grooms have been wearing hired white wedding gowns and ordinary lounge suits, respectively, at their weddings for at least a generation. The traditional regional clothing, the short white ballet-like skirts for men and the long dresses with embroidered vests for women, are now worn only by the school children in the playlets they present on patriotic occasions.

Men's outer clothing today follows the standard European style of dark lounge suit, shirt, socks, and low oxfords. The middle-aged and older farmers avoid wearing neckties even on special occasions, since these stand for urban professional occupations. Some of the younger farmers did wear neckties for Easter in 1956 and were strongly criticized for doing so. The young men of the village dress much as their elders do, except that they make an effort to keep up with changing urban styles in coat-sweaters and shirts. Only one man in the village wears a fedora hat, a sign of leisure in Vasilika. The rest of the men, when they wear any head covering at all, wear cloth peaked caps. Winter overcoats are also of standard European style. The same type of clothing is used by men for work in the fields. They merely save old clothes for the purpose and wear a sweater instead of a suit jacket. Older men wear long woolen underwear all through the year. The young men and boys do not—they work in shirt sleeves more frequently than the older men do. Except for overcoats and sweaters, men wear the same kind of clothing thoughout the year.

There is a slightly greater variation in women's clothing patterns, based on age as well as on income. Women in their forties or older wear dark blue homespun skirts with long-sleeved blouses and woolen cloth shawls for warmth. They always wear long lisle stockings and cloth slippers. A brown kerchief, wound around so that it forms a kind of close-fitting cap or helmet, is rarely removed by these women—one even wore it in bed throughout a hospital stay. Under the brown kerchief their hair is left long and dressed in braids around the head. Over the brown kerchief, for work around the house or in the fields, these women put on an additional kerchief, usually white in color, which is loosely tied under the chin for most kinds of work. They pull the ends around to cover their mouths when they do heavy work in the fields. In Vasilika, the colors of the outer kerchief indicate only whether or not a woman is in mourning. Black kerchiefs (and black clothes in general) are a sign that a woman is in mourning for a close relative; dark-colored kerchiefs indicate that she is in mourning for a more distant relative. The village women also associate the outer kerchief with their status as rural women who work in the fields.

Many observers have assumed that the practice of drawing the kerchief in front of the face to cover the mouth has the same meaning as the Muslim practice of veiling their women. It may be that the style of draping the kerchiefs was taken up during the Turkish occupation, but in contemporary Vasilika it has none of the connotation of modesty, it rather signifies work—specifically labor in the fields. The women explain the use of the outer kerchief in entirely utilitarian terms. They say it keeps the dust out of their mouths.

Women and girls under forty have a different style of dress. In winter, on ordinary days both indoors and out, they wear cotton flannel, printed kimono-like garments with long sleeves. They wear lisle stockings and cloth slippers with the kimonos. The girls prefer bright colors, with red often the favorite. In summer, the younger women wear cotton or rayon summer dresses which are of generalized European style. The younger women never wear the helmet-like brown inner kerchief, though they wear the outer kerchief, in the fields. Their hair is cut short. The last of the younger generation of girls over sixteen still wearing braids in 1955 cut her hair in 1956 in time for Easter. The kimono, the short hair, the discarding of the inner kerchief, are all recognized as signs of progress in the village. Many of these younger women are eager to have permanent waves when a traveling beautician comes through the settlement.

The oldest women and the least prosperous among the younger women of the village dress on holidays as they do every other day—they own no dress clothes, as it were, but the unmarried girls of all income levels try to manage something new, including, if possible, a pair of nylon stockings. What it will be is kept a secret, and Easter outfits are often sewed late at night, or tried on in real seclusion, so that other families will not see what the girls will wear until the day itself.

Except for the winter kimonos, clothes are acquired only for holidays, and then, after a few months, become everyday clothes to wear when working around the house or in the fields. In consequence, wool dresses or rayon clothes lose their shapes; the seams split and tear, because these garments were not originally designed to withstand the strenuous work the women do in them. Both men's and women's clothes get badly soiled from the fields, and they are washed in hot water and often pounded with a paddle as well, to loosen all the dirt. The homespun fabrics of the older women withstand such treatment well, but the wools and rayons of the younger women and the men's suits rather quickly reach the condition of old rags, as the villagers call them, and thereby become suitable for work in the fields and around the house.

Children's clothing has become important for the villagers because the standard of what is expected has changed within the last two decades. One farmer and his wife explained their desire not to have more than the two children they already had by saying that, among other things, their children now had to have shoes all the time, a requirement which did not exist when they themselves were children. In the winter, some children wear rubbers over heavy stockings but without shoes. Boys wear short pants until late adolescence, but otherwise their clothes are like those of their elders. Girls wear dresses like those of the younger women. Kimonos, however, are not considered appropriate for schoolgirls. Since the same clothing is usually worn indoors and out during the winter, small boys and girls wear cotton pinafores over their outer coats in order to prevent too fast soiling. Some mothers knit sweaters for their children, but gloves are not worn for warmth either by children or by adults. Uncomfortably cold hands are expected throughout the winter, and during this season, as they enter a house, people frequently walk directly to the front of the fire and extend their hands towards the flame. Some of the young girls wear thin gloves, for show rather than for warmth, when they go to church. Children, like their parents, are now expected to have new clothes at Easter, and, if possible, for other holidays as well. They must be neatly dressed for school. A few of Vasilika's children wear torn, patched, faded clothing out of economic necessity.

Urbanity vs. Convenience

The urban acquisitions relieve some of the work load and add to the variety of life, and the villagers frequently express satisfaction at having the new conveniences and the new relief from boredom. But convenience seems to be welcomed less for its own sake than as a by-product of goods and practices that are primarily valued for their air of urban sophistication, of "progress." For example, most of the wells in the village have no windlasses to ease the labor of bringing up the pails full of water. Women simply keep a rope attached to a pail, lower the pail into the well, and use the rope to lift it out again, hand over hand. The water level in many of the wells is low, so that drawing a pail of water is hard physical labor which must be done at least twice a day, but the women did not agitate for windlasses in the way they did for cement basins, for obviously, windlasses have no urban cachet about them. They do want running water in the homes—an urbanism—and it will, incidentally, relieve them of the drudgery of drawing so much well-water, but for a generation, the presence of a few windlasses in the village did not inspire other families to acquire them.

The overt recognition on the part of the villagers that they admire and accept the new items because they stand for progress and sophistication and not entirely for whatever utility they may have is exemplified by the comment of one of Vasilika's less prosperous inhabitants whose living conditions were among the least favorable in the village. His house did, in 1959, have electricity, however, and he had one naked bulb hanging in the center of his one small upstairs room. This man described for us his feelings about a recent visit he had made to the *paniyiri* of a mountain village which had no electricity. "I couldn't stay there more than a day," he said. "They had no electric light, and I cannot live like that any more. I have become a European," he concluded, with a smile, using the term that Greeks use for the inhabitants of Europe west of the Adriatic.

A second reason for the acceptance of new uses for cash is simply the rivalry among Vasilika's families. If one family with urban connections has something new, other families make an effort to get the same thing. One of the effects of the process is that some families whose incomes barely enable them to subsist sometimes use their meager cash resources on plastic tablecloths or new clothes, as a token of their participation in the battle for prestige.

One important characteristic of the changes in the villagers' consumption habits is that virtually all the substitutions and additions require the villagers to dip into their cash resources. In this respect, the new needs act as a spur to the cash crop economy of the settlement and provide motivation for more efficient farming. Increased efficiency in farming adds to income and it becomes possible to finance still more innovations. The extent to which this kind of interrelated process can continue is, of course, dependent on world markets for the villagers' produce, on the level of economic activity in the entire Greek nation, and, more specifically, on the extent to which the population no longer needed on the farms can be productively employed in the towns and cities. The inheritance and dowry system of Vasilika's residents is central to this matter and is the subject of the next chapter.

4

The Family: Dowry and Inheritance; Formal Structure[1]

T HE DOWRY AND INHERITANCE SYSTEM in Vasilika is primarily a mechanism by which property is transferred from one generation to the next. It is this kind of mechanism, but it is also more. By reason of the context of values in which they operate and because of their specific characteristics, dowry and inheritance patterns as they function in Vasilika have ramifications not only for the Boeotian countryside but also for Greece as a whole.

Inheritance by Sons

Both the Greek laws of inheritance and village custom require that property be divided equally among all the children, sons and daughters alike. Some receive their shares through inheritance or by gifts while the parents are still alive, but the daughters of a family are entitled to their share at marriage in the form of a dowry. Since, from the standpoint of the villagers, a man's most compelling obligation is to arrange for the successful marriage of his daughters, and since no girl in Vasilika can normally expect to marry without at least a token dowry, the girls have first lien on the family's property. For most of Vasilika's families, land holdings are the most valuable assets, and dowries are, therefore, calculated ordinarily as a transfer of a share of the land from parents to a daughter and through her to the jurisdiction of her husband. However, if a family's land holdings are such that it is obvious that by giving daughters their

[1] Portions of this chapter were presented as a paper at a conference on Rural Peoples of the Mediterranean held at Burg Wartenstein in July 1959, and will appear in *Mediterranean Countrymen*, edited by Julian Pitt-Rivers, Mouton and Co., The Hague, scheduled for publication in 1962.

share of the land at the time of their marriage, the shares remaining for the sons will be too small to enable them to support their future wives and children, the family recognizes the problem and tries to make some adjustment that will prevent the threatened poverty. The villagers are well aware of the dangers of land fragmentation under a system of equal inheritance. The average land holding in Vasilika is already only one-third to one-fourth of what it was at the time the village was settled. Thanks to the introduction of irrigation and improvements in agricultural techniques (see Chapters 2 and 3), both the bulk of yields and the cash value of the crops in the area have increased to the point at which the farmers maintain a higher standard of living on the smaller holdings than their grandfathers did on the more extensive ones. But the process has its limits, and the future possibility of economically useless small holdings is a real hazard for Vasilika's families.

One kind of solution to its problem is for a family to try to train or educate its "surplus" sons for a nonfarming occupation; if possible, one that will send them to the towns and cities as white-collar workers or as professional men. This effort, however, is more than merely a solution to a recognized problem. Status as an urbanite has very high value for the villagers in its own right. As the previous chapter has shown, the families of Vasilika try to import urban ways into the village; their efforts to send their own sons and daughters directly into the towns and cities may now be discussed. For quite apart from the necessities of their situation, the people of Vasilika act as if they assumed that life in towns and cities is superior to life in a small village. This judgment is not based on a belief that there is necessarily greater economic well-being in the towns. On the contrary, the villagers believe it is more difficult to achieve a respectable standard in the larger centers and, indeed, that the plight of the poor is worse in the town than in the village. They say it is harder to have little when one is tempted by so much. But the villagers respect an educated man; education enables a person to pursue occupations which the villagers believe have greater prestige than farming, and the preponderance of these occupations are practiced in towns. Not only white-collar workers but also journalists, lawyers, doctors, writers, gymnasium and university professors congregate in the provincial towns and in Athens (cf. Antonakaki 1955:93). Even if a young man from Vasilika is not fortunate enough to work in one of these favored occupations—even if he is a tailor or a barber or an artisan of another type, or a small merchant—he is believed to acquire some aura of prestige simply by living in the more populous center.

The young girls of Vasilika want to marry into the towns because they are well aware of the greater physical ease and comfort available there and contrast these conditions favorably with the arduous and endless labor they are accustomed to in the village.

Still another incentive for gaining the status of a town dweller is the belief, in Vasilika, that life in town is more full of adventure and less monotonous than life in the village. Besides, the towns and Athens have crowds, and *polis cosmos* (many people) are enjoyed by the villagers for their own sake. A *paniyiri* or Easter is considered successful in proportion to the number of people the village attracts, and the villagers comment on their satisfaction at seeing some different faces.

A caveat may be in order here, however. No matter how much the villagers like the variety of life in the towns, and no matter how much they dislike the tiring and messy work on the farms, when they actually live in the village and are engaged in the work in the fields and at home, they work hard, steadily, and with a will. The people of Vasilika do not believe work is ennobling in itself; they seem to have no compulsive need to work to achieve self-respect, but they accept the need for hard labor as a means to the end of support for the family. Therefore, the villagers expect the farmer and his household to work hard and for long hours if an agricultural existence is their immediate fate, but do not condemn some farmer if he tries to arrange a different fate for his children. If he is unsuccessful, and all his sons stay on the farm, or if his daughters are married off to farmers, there is no disgrace in that either, as long as he did the best he could. And if a farmer can bequeath a good farm to any of his sons and the son manages the property skillfully, the economic success of the farm brings a measure of prestige, in Vasilika, to father and son alike.

Within the context of these values let us consider how the dowry and inheritance system functions in Vasilika. Sometimes after a farmer marries and has had at least one child, it would appear that he and his wife consider the question of how many more children it would be sensible for them to have. The parents recognize that the more children they have, the harder it will be to provide adequately for the future of each of them. Therefore, regulation of the size of families is accepted in the village as obviously prudent and sensible. The villagers explain that more children survive nowadays as a result of modern medical care, and that this obviates the need to have a large family in the hope that at least two or three of the children will reach maturity. In Vasilika, some prenatal care and confinement in one of the proprietary hospitals in Levadhia is recognized now as the safest kind of maternity care and also has the most prestige (Friedl 1958). Such care immediately increases the cost of childbirth and is a drain on the family's resources. But even those families whose babies are born at home with the aid of a traveling government-trained midwife are expected, as we have seen, to provide better food and finer clothing for their children than earlier generations provided for theirs. The added expense of rearing children has not been counterbalanced by any increase in their economic value on the farms. On the contrary, less labor is regularly needed, as Chapter 2 has shown.

The trend to smaller families seems to have started back in the 1920's. Genealogies show that the parents of the marriageable young adults of the middle and late 1950's had already limited the size of their families to a mode of four children in contrast to their parents who typically had had eight. The overt statements made by married men and women of all ages including the sixty- and seventy-year-old widows indicate that the change is deliberate and coincides with their expressed attitudes. Parents who have more children than they can adequately feed and care for are accused of behaving like animals; they are said to have neither brains nor self-control. Parents with marriageable children were, therefore, in 1961, contemplating the division of their estates into fewer portions than their parents had done before them.

As his children are growing up, a farmer calculates approximately what he must give his daughter or daughters for dowries and how much will be left for each of his sons to share. If it is fairly obvious that the share left for the sons will be insufficient to support each of them, the farmer tries to make some other provision for one or more of the boys. Any boy who shows promise as a student is encouraged to continue his schooling beyond the compulsory sixth-grade elementary school in the village. Education is so highly prized that sometimes even an only son who might inherit an adequate farm is allowed to continue his education if he shows ability in academic subjects. The next step after elementary school most commonly chosen by the villagers is the six-year classical or humanistic gymnasium which serves as a necessary base for any civil service or white-collar post, and also for further study in the university or in specialized advanced technical schools. Although there are some private gymnasia, most of the farmers of Vasilika have sent their sons to the virtually free public institutions (Antonakaki 1955:39). These are in the provincial towns or in Athens, so that although there is little tuition charge, the farmer must pay for his son's board and room, for his school supplies, and for adequate clothing. Whenever possible, children are boarded with an aunt or uncle who lives in the town, but even under these conditions, farmers pay a fee to the relatives to cover the cost of their children's care. Sometimes, to keep food costs down, a mother prepares a basket of bread, cheese, and perhaps a vegetable stew for her son, places it in the bus bound for the town in which the boy goes to school, and the boy picks up the basket at the bus depot.

Whatever the particular arrangement, schooling involves an expenditure of current income, and the farmers consider that the cost of educating a son is about equivalent to a major portion of his share of the inheritance. The Greek Civil Code makes a specific provision for this view by declaring that educational expenses beyond those normally to be expected from the economic position of the family may be counted as part of the inheritance (Section 1895). In Vasilika it is assumed that a gymnasium-educated young man will spend the rest of his life living in some town, and that he will receive only a token share of the land after his father's death or at the time of the division of the estate. His parents, brothers, and sisters remaining in the villages as farmers gain in social stature and in potential actual advantage from his residence in town in a prestige-giving occupation. Both the legal code and village custom, then, involve the recognition that when farmers or shepherds undertake to educate their sons beyond the village school, they are striving for an improved status position in the nation as a whole, and that if sons succeed in the new prestige-giving occupation, they are the agents of upward social mobility for the family. Among Vasilika's land-owning farmers, an educated son gives the village the added advantage of a larger amount of land to divide among the remaining children. For farmers and shepherds who have very small land holdings or none at all, the sacrifices necessary to keep an academically talented son in the gymnasium are undertaken with enthusiasm, because such a son gives promise both of increasing the income of his family and of raising its social position.

Although not all of Vasilika's boys who start the gymnasium have sufficient talent or self-discipline to complete the course, a majority of them do so and give observable evidence of the feasibility of sending boys for advanced schooling. In 1959, of the thirty-four boys and young men who were between the ages of twelve and thirty and who were also sons of farmers, sixteen had attended or were then attending gymnasium, and three of the sixteen had received or were still receiving some education at a higher level. By 1961, as we have seen, a shepherd's boy had completed a year in gymnasium. Whether all these sons will succeed in finding employment commensurate with their educational qualifications depends, of course, on the economic development of the nation, and especially on the increased possibilities for employment in the towns and in Athens. In Vasilika each educated young man and his family hope that he will not have to return to the village to live.

The pattern of educating sons is not a new one in the village. With few exceptions, the groups of middle-aged brothers and of young adult brothers and sisters in the village in 1961 could boast of one additional brother who was living in a town or in Athens, and each of these men had had some education beyond the village school. There were also two men in this age group who were living in the village but had had some gymnasium training.

A second solution to the problem of surplus sons well known in the history of Greece has been emigration out of the country itself. In the decade between 1910 and 1920 about four young men left Vasilika for the United States. One of these returned to fight in the Balkan Wars of 1912 and has lived in the village ever since. The other three are still in the United States. In the 1930's, one man left with his wife and child for Tanganyika. The extent of continuing association with these overseas relatives is different in each case; one man returned to Vasilika to visit his brother in the early 1950's and stayed for only a year; another wrote sporadically; a third disappeared and his son knew only that he had died in the States. The Tanganyika relatives, however, continually sent packages to their village cousins, and the son of the original emigré, who had died, returned to the village with his mother in 1959. The villagers always referred to the packages from Tanganyika as gifts from America and referred to the Tanganyikan, even after his return, as "the American." Apparently, the word "America" in the village is a generic term for an El Dorado abroad. However, emigration out of the country is not currently of interest to the villagers; no one in the village ever asked us for help in arranging the emigration of one of their sons to the United States, though joking references to our taking young people back with us were not uncommon.

Up to this point, then, we may conclude that the system of equal inheritance of property and the villagers' approval of urban living have led to an actual geographical movement of young men out of Vasilika and to a social movement into occupations other than farming for young men who have grown up in the rural settlement. Another aspect of the situation is that income from land directly supports boys who live in towns both during their years in school and until they find a job. The possible importance of this for the urban economy of Greece will be discussed again in connection with dower wealth that is transferred to the cities.

Dowering the Daughter

The dowry shall be discussed first as the social mechanism by which daughters inherit property at marriage, and second as a mechanism for social mobility. In Vasilika, parents are obligated to arrange marriages for their children, and with few exceptions they do so. They most frequently look for spouses outside of the village. They expect that a girl will leave the village to live with her husband and that a farming son will bring his wife to Vasilika to live with him (technically, patrilocal residence). In Vasilika, when the villagers speak of the engagement of a man or a woman, they say, "He (she) has become engaged in Mirali;" or in Sfaka, or in Athens, or in whatever village or town the prospective spouse comes from. They explain the prevalence of exogamy, to which the phrase just quoted gives linguistic expression, by saying that it is too difficult to find, inside Vasilika, anyone who is sufficiently distantly related to be eligible for marriage.

The custom of the village prohibits marriage between relatives on both the mother's and father's side to the degree of third cousin. In a village with a total population of 216, in which there are six sets of adult brothers and one group of three men whose fathers were brothers, there will certainly be limits to the number of boys and girls eligible to marry each other. The number of families connected by kin ties in the village is even larger, however, because in each generation there are some marriages that do take place among fellow villagers and this, of course, relates some of the village's children to each other through their mother's line, even if their fathers have no paternal relatives in Vasilika. Kinship connections are further extended within the village by the ceremonial kinship ties of godparenthood. On the ground that any godparental relationship between two individuals automatically places not only the individuals concerned but both their elementary families into close kin relations, the Greek Orthodox Church prohibits marriages between the two families to the same degree that would be necessary if they were consanguineal; that is, blood relatives.

When a daughter is to be married, the father of the girl is believed to have ultimate responsibility for giving the dowry. However, the brothers' interests are involved, the mother is deeply concerned about the future of her daughter, and certainly the girl herself wants to know something about her prospects. In the informal discussions that go on within the family, everyone participates and expresses his point of view. The father alone, however, has the formal responsibility for conducting the negotiations, which are always carried on with the aid of a *proksenitis* or *proksinitra* (marriage intermediary). In the Boeotian countryside, this person (either a man or a woman) is a friend or relative, either from the village or from the community of the prospective spouse, rather than a professional. On the groom's side, the father participates in the negotiations, but the prospective groom himself is present and active in the proceedings. His decision as to the minimum value of the dowry and the form in which he will accept it is the crucial one.

The dowry negotiations and the final marriage contract can be usefully discussed, therefore, as analogous to a commercial transaction in which each side tries to get the most value at the least cost. For the bride's father, the material costs include the land and cash he must give as part of his daughter's dowry. She is, of course, legally and customarily entitled to her share of the patrimony, but except for the cash, the determination of just how much is her share is not easy to arrive at. A farmer, as we have seen, holds land in scattered parcels of different quality; some of the parcels are in the immediate vicinity of Vasilika, no more than an hour's walk away from the village; others may have been part of his wife's dowry and may, therefore, be near her village; his house has value, but since his daughter will not live with him, he cannot give her part of it. The problem is solved in Vasilika by making a rough estimate of the money value of the parents' property in terms of gold sovereigns (*lires*) and then determining how many *lires* a girl is entitled to. Since the end of the Greek Civil War in 1949, the drachma has been stabilized, and the villagers as well as the rest of the Greek population are gaining confidence in the currency. However, the belief that gold sovereigns, worth approximately $10 each in 1961, are the only trustworthy form of cash is still common in Greece, as is the hoarding of the sovereigns and the requirement that bills be paid in them. The villagers evaluate property in terms of *lires* and always speak of a dowry as one of so many *lires,* regardless of whether the property transferred is cash or land or both.

Besides the property costs of the dowry, a farmer loses the labor of his daughter both on the farm and in the household. Finally, there is an emotional cost to the parents, particularly to the mother, at the marriage of a daughter. A mother loses the companionship of a friend, a confidante, and a working partner in the house and the fields. Among the more prosperous farmers, girls marry in their middle or late twenties. As a result mothers frequently have had many years of cooperation with grown daughters. The wrench at parting is seriously felt. Mothers in Vasilika openly lament the loss of their daughters and speak frequently of how much they miss their absent girls.

When a marriage is contemplated between families of equal wealth and social position, for example, when the daughter of a farmer is being married to a man who expects to stay on his father's farm, and when his share of the farm has approximately the same value as what the girl brings in as a dowry, the negotiations are relatively straightforward. Each side can then limit itself to checking on the claims the other is making and to surveying the total situation. Is the yield of the land the girl is bringing what her father says it is? Will the son-in-law be entitled to the share of the land he claims he will have? Does the boy have so many sisters that his father may die before they have been married off leaving the boy with the responsibility of dowering them? Is the father-in-law's house well enough equipped so that the girl will be able to live at approximately the standard she had at home? How many brothers does the groom have who are also going to be farmers and who will, therefore, have to share the house itself, or for whom some housing provision must eventually be made? Because personal qualities of the prospective groom will influence the success with which he manages his own and his dower properties, a father asks whether the groom has a reputation for industriousness. Is there any danger that the groom will "eat" the dowry properties, as the villagers phrase a propensity for using capital resources for current needs or for luxuries? Are the groom's father and brothers sober men who will conserve property and work to get the best income from it?

In short, the bride's father wants to assure, insofar as he is able, the future well-being of his daughter and of her children. He also wants the emotional satisfaction of having been successful at making a good arrangement for her. One village father pointed to a field we were passing and explained that he had given it to his daughter as part of her *prika* (dowry), so that all the cotton from the field was for his grandson. He then went on to say that he had married his daughter well and said of his three-year-old grandson, "Who knows, one day he might become a lawyer or a doctor. He has a brain, the little one." The implication was that he, the farmer, had contributed to whatever the final destiny of his grandson might be by having supplied such good fields for his daughter's dowry.

A girl's parents also want assurance that she will live in a congenial household. They hope that the new mother-in-law and the groom's sisters will accept the girl with good grace and that she will be decently treated. A man's wife and daughter will always remind him of the resources the family has already expended on the trousseau and the skill with which they were woven. From the women's point of view, these are important parts of the cost, and they want a girl to go to a family which will appreciate both the quantity and the fine workmanship of the *rukha*. Some friction between a girl and her mother-in-law and sisters-in-law is accepted in Vasilika as part of the condition of marriage to a farmer. The severity of friction is mitigated, however, by the independent dignity a girl acquires by having brought her husband a dowry and by the pride her husband's family takes in their own skill at having helped arrange a good marriage for their son.

The groom's interest, on the other hand, is to supplement his patrimony with as much land and cash as he can get from his wife's dowry. After their marriage, the husband and wife will have jurisdiction over her dowry properties. Unless the marriage contract states otherwise, and it rarely does in marriages between a farmer and a village girl, the husband has the right to the management and control of movable and personal property that he received with his wife and the management of the real estate given as part of the dowry. The alienation of movable dower property requires only the informal consent of his wife, while the alienation of real estate requires a formal notarized consent statement from his wife and the permission of the court (Civil Code Sections 1416 and 1417). (The groom's father, therefore, is interested only from the standpoint of the general welfare of his son. He himself will have no direct control over his daughter-in-law's land or money.) From the groom's point of view, an industrious young girl also has high value, and if she is healthy, good-looking, modest, virtuous, and amiable as well, she is of still additional worth. Therefore, an ugly older girl with a bad reputation would have to bring a large dowry to compensate for her personal deficiencies. Conversely, an attractive, healthy, virtuous young girl might be able to marry a slightly wealthier man than her dowry would normally be expected to command. Greek folk songs often lament the story of a young girl who attracted a wealthy older suitor to whom her family married her because he was willing to take a smaller dowry. The songs, in this instance, reflect actual situations known on the Boeotian countryside, although they do not occur with any great frequency.

Negotiations, Courtship, and Marriage

For the families involved, the marriage negotiations have the quality of participation in a kind of ritualized contest. A young man may have been recommended to a girl's father; the father sends an intermediary with information as to how much dowry he is willing to give; the intermediary then goes off to the groom and his father, to whom he exaggerates the size of the dowry and the qualities of the girl. The villagers assume he will also exaggerate the qualities of the groom to the girl's family. The enjoyment of the game lies in each group's efforts indirectly to get accurate information about the other side. This is done by making inquiries among one's own relatives living in the prospective spouse's village and by asking questions of others who know the family. Secrecy about the very existence of the negotiations is helpful at this point, because the villagers do not believe they can get accurate information if anyone knows they have a direct interest in the matter. Many times a sister in another village will act as informal intermediary for her brother and try to find out how much of a dowry some of the better young men are asking for. Tentative questions of this sort may be asked for years before a serious negotiation is finally fully launched. These tentative steps may be terminated at any time without loss of honor on either side if the young man informs the intermediary that the dowry is not quite enough, or if the girl's father uses the excuse that his daughter is not yet ready to marry because she has not accumulated sufficient *rukha*. In fact, the grooms are not interested in the *rukha*. As one villager phrased it, "It is land and money they burn for around here."

In Vasilika, both in the previous generations and at present, it has been possible for a young man and woman never to have seen each other until the first formal occasion for meeting. However, a young man may have seen an attractive girl at a *paniyiri* or other festival, and may have asked his father to investigate her situation. But, since unmarried village boys and girls do not talk to each other in public unless they are related, the chances are that he has never talked to her. A young girl may, in her turn, know a great deal about the young men in the surrounding villages and may also have had opportunities to see them at the local festivities, but may never have talked to any of them. In any case, it is village custom for both boy and girl to act as if they know nothing about the discussions going on. At the first formal meeting, both the boy and girl have the right to express any personal antipathy they may have for the prospective spouse. But if the marriage is otherwise an advantageous one, they are likely to be persuaded to overcome any but the most extreme feelings of repugnance. The villagers are not callous about the matter of personal compatibility between spouses; they assume, however, that if the marriage conditions are right, a harmonious relationship will develop, and if it does not, the successful economic or prestige conditions of the marriage will help to allay sufferings arising from the lack of personal contentment.

Once the major provisions of the marriage contract are agreed upon, the machinery for the formal engagement gets under way. This involves, first, a visit by the groom, his father, and several of his other relatives, but not his mother, to the home of the bride. Here the men again check on the agreements, the father of the groom pins a single *lira* on the bride, the bride's mother pins a *lira* on the groom; there is food and drink, and the bride gives gifts of small items such as socks, stockings, pillow cases, or towels to the groom and his entire group. For the women, this process is important; what is given on the one hand, and what is received on the other, is discussed by the women on both sides with great zest and frequent criticism. If this affair raises no issues which lead to the dissolution of the agreements, about ten days later, the bride's father invites his own relatives and those of the groom from wherever they are in Greece to a large engagement party which lasts from a Saturday night through to Sunday. The bride's neighbors and the groom's friends also come.

From the time of the ceremonial exchange of the *lires,* the young couple are considered formally engaged. They are now free not only to see each other but to travel anywhere together, and the groom may even come and stay at the girl's home for some time. In the villagers' view, if the young couple have proper respect for both sets of parents they will refrain from sex relations during this period. Certainly if the girl becomes pregnant before the wedding there is disapproval not only because of the moral stigma, but also because it requires an immediate wedding at a time when the accumulation of the agreed-upon dowry property may not yet have been completed. A premature ceremony is therefore not advantageous to the groom. Engagements lasting a year or more are frequent, and the villagers speak of unfortunate situations in which this status has been protracted for as long as ten years.

Weddings in Vasilika in recent years, the villagers say, have become less elaborate and less of a village event than they once were. As later sections will show, many of the village girls marry men in the towns, and this frequently results in having the wedding in the town church rather than in Vasilika. Moreover, the villagers say, this system obviates the necessity of inviting large numbers of villagers to the wedding feast and so cuts down on the cost to the bride's father.

At weddings held in the village between children of farmers, however, much of the tradition is maintained. For example, the groom's male relatives come to the house of the bride on the Saturday afternoon before the Sunday wedding to take the *rukha* and the house furnishings she has received as gifts to the groom's home. The groom hires a truck to do the job, not because there is so much furniture, but because of the quantity of *rukha*. A Vasilika girl is expected to have woven at home approximately thirty sheets, six light blankets, two heavy woolen carpets, five lighter woolen floor coverings, five coarse woolen blankets, four mattress covers, ten carry-all bags or sacks, two heavy ornamental table covers, one red-and-white striped and one blue-and-white striped tablecloth with twelve napkins to match each of the cloths, six cotton face towels, and two long cotton towels for the tray in which loaves of bread are left to rise before baking. To this accumulation she will add several pieces that are bought from itinerant merchants and embroidered at home. Also purchased, usually in town, are white sheets, pillow cases, and turkish towels as well as the material for about six pairs of curtains. Furniture consisting of a wooden wardrobe, a bed, a table, and some chairs may be added, as are the cooking and serving utensils given to the girl as gifts. The colorful collection fills a small pick-up truck, and the sight of one of these on the road with laughing and singing young men crowding whatever space is left is a sure sign of a wedding. On Sunday morning the groom's party, including his marriage sponsor (*kumbaros*), arrive at the house of the bride. The *kumbaros* leads the group to the house, only to find the door closed and locked. He begs that the door be opened. The girls inside giggle and demand 1,000 drachmas to open the door. After some bargaining, the *kumbaros* gives a five-drachma piece and the party comes in. It is the *kumbaros* who rents the bride's white wedding gown, provides the wedding crowns, the large white candles which are held at the ceremony, and the *kufeta,* the sugar covered almonds arranged in small packages of white netting, tied with a white ribbon, which he distributes to each of the guests after the ceremony. After the wedding feast, for which musicians are hired so that the guests can sing and dance, the bride is accompanied to the groom's home by her brothers and sometimes a sister. The women, including the bride, all cry as they leave the girl with her new husband.[2] But even among farmers these customs are changing, and in recent years the bride and groom have taken to leaving the wedding guests to go off on a short honeymoon.

Disposition of Dower Property

After the marriage of a farmer, the couple is settled in the man's village, usually in the home of his parents. The groom has acquired some parcels of land in his wife's village and a small hoard of cash as well. For the first few years of his marriage, he may go to his wife's village to work the land himself, or he may contract with his father-in-law or with one of his brothers-in-law to work it for him on shares. Either way he will have occasion to visit his wife's village and to have some association with her father and brothers. In the meantime, he is likely to be looking for an opportunity to exchange land with a farmer who

---

[2] The description of the engagement and wedding ceremonies is not complete. The details selected are meant to give only an impression of the nature of these affairs.

lives in his wife's village and has married a girl from his own settlement and, therefore, has land near the groom's village. A farmer husband may even be willing to consider the sale of the land in his wife's village to make a good purchase nearer home. Neither of these possibilities may come to fruition for years, so that they may remain subjects for long-term discussion between a man and his father- and brothers-in-law. To summarize the situation, land given as one part of the dowry and village exogamy have the consequence of stimulating land exchanges and sales in the Boeotian countryside, of stimulating the visits of men among the villages in the region with a consequent exchange of views and ideas, and of providing an economic focus for maintaining some kind of relationships between affinal relatives, that is relatives by marriage. The system of transferring land as dowry has the effect also of permitting a man to utilize his wife's property throughout his married life instead of having to wait to do so until after his wife's father's death.

The actions of the villagers and the tone in which they discuss these questions suggest that although there is some sentiment attached to the land inherited from a father and to the land that were parts of a mother's dowry, the symbolic value of particular parcels of land as a link between generations does not usually take precedence over the economic value of the land as an income and food producer.

We have still to consider the question of the ultimate disposition of dower properties in marriages between farmers. The Greek Civil Code states that dower property must be accounted for separately from that owned or eventually inherited by the husband, and as we have seen, stipulates that the consent of the wife is required before dower property can be sold or exchanged. If there is a divorce, the wife is entitled to the return of the dower property or of its equivalent. In the house of the groom's father, the newly married couple is given a room in which they and, later, their children sleep. Here the bride's trousseau gives the room a personal touch. Both the young people work on the farm holdings of the groom's father along with his father, mother, and brothers, and unmarried sisters. They also work on the young wife's dower lands. The income from these may be pooled with that from the paternal holdings but need not be. The young husband's father has jurisdiction over the ordinary living expenses of the entire household and distributes the cash needed for purchases of clothing, food, and household equipment. During the lifetime of his father, the cash portion of the dowry may be invested by the son in additional land or in some other capital equipment such as a diesel pump. Under no circumstances do the villagers consider it proper to sell dower lands or to use dower funds for ordinary living expenses. Only the need for money for a very serious illness or for some other emergency is felt to justify such action. In whatever form, the dowry is considered capital which may be invested or saved to add to the estate available for the newly married couple's children.

After the death of the husband's father, the young man continues to live with his brothers, most of whom are likely to be married by now, until they decide to separate and divide the patrimony. This now consists of the property their father inherited from his father's patrimony, the dower property of their mother, and any additional properties acquired by their father in the course of his lifetime.

Division of the Patrimony

The division of the property is always a dramatic event in the lives of the villagers. They believe that the separation of brothers is necessitated more by human than by economic considerations. They explain that brothers should be able to get along with each other and work together under the supervision of the eldest. Harmonious relations between brothers are highly approved in the village, and their maintenance is considered a moral obligation. But, the villagers will add, "What can you do?" When the wives and children of several brothers are part of the same household, inevitably they quarrel. One wife complains that her children's shoes are all worn out while her nieces and nephews are wearing new shoes. The matter of the work contributions to the joint household causes dissension; each wife tries to convince her husband that he works harder than the others. The children of one brother may cry at night and keep another brother and his wife from getting proper sleep. There also may be some envy if the dowry received by one brother is larger than that of the others.

The decision to divide the property may be delayed in spite of considerable disharmony in the household for several reasons. First, division implies a kind of moral defeat. Second, there are economic factors which favor the maintenance of a joint household. It cuts down on the consumption expenditures for each of the families; more women are released for work in the fields because the young children may be cared for at home by the grandmother or by only one of the wives; and the amount invested in farm animals and equipment can be held down because they are cooperatively used. Then, too, as one farmer puts it, before brothers divide the patrimony, it seems as if they have a lot of land and are earning a good living, but once the property is divided, each brother has little and then one sees that the family was not so wealthy after all. Appearances are important to the villagers, and a group of brothers may be reluctant to reveal the details of their economic condition. But the most important impediment to the separation of the brothers is the house itself. For the house is part of the patrimony, and if the brothers separate, the housing must also somehow be divided among them. There are several ways in which the villagers have solved this last problem.

When there are only two brothers involved, the house may be physically divided simply by building a wall between two sets of rooms both upstairs and downstairs. The brothers work together to improve both parts of the house so that each is of equal value and then draw lots to determine which brother gets which part (Levy 1956). Such houses are thenceforth called *dhipla* (double houses), and two or more families live in them as in entirely different establishments. Once the households are separated, a brother who has received cash in his wife's dowry is now able to make further improvements in his side of the house without regard for the other. There were four double houses in Vasilika in 1961.

None were then occupied by brothers; their occupants were second and third generation descendants of the brothers who had originally put in the wall. The houses showed the effects of the long separation. In one of the houses, one side has been inhabited by a branch of the family that is losing its lands; that side has no additions and is in poor repair. The descendants of the other brother have prospered and have added some rooms and a terrace to their side of the house. In another case, both parts of the house have been expanded and modernized but in different ways.

Vasilika's houses are not ordinarily large enough to be divided into more than two parts. If there are more than two brothers, or if the paternal house is small, another solution to the housing problem exists. Here, the brothers agree to refurnish the ancestral house which one of them will continue to inhabit, and to build, in addition, new houses to the number of the remaining farmer brothers. The significance of the agreement is that the cost of the new houses and the repair and modernization of the old will be borne by the patrimony. Moreover, the brothers do not decide in advance which one is to have which house. That decision is made by drawing lots after the new houses are habitable and the old one has been improved. In a sense, the brothers agree jointly to improve the father's estate before they take their shares. The process is not different from that involved when the men in a joint household buy land which is added to the estate and is eventually divided among them. The process of building the new houses takes years (in one case where two new houses were built, the actual work took seven years) and during that time the brothers and their wives watch carefully to make sure that no one house is less well equipped than any other; for no man knows which of the houses it will fall to his lot to own.

The drawing of lots and thereby the division of the property does not have to await the completion of the new houses. As in the towns and cities in Greece, a dwelling is considered habitable at what to an American view is an early stage in its construction. Villagers will live in a house in which the ground-level rooms still have earthen floors, in which there is no ceiling to hide the rafters and to exclude the earth and dust that the wind sends through the roof, in which only the outer stone walls have been completed and the inner walls have not yet been plastered or stuccoed. Even at that, the cost of labor and materials for the basic stone or brick shell of a two-story house in Vasilika can absorb the surplus cash from joint holding of some eighty *stremata* for two or three years.

Once it is agreed that the new houses are ready for occupancy and that the old house has been sufficiently improved, the moment for the separation has come. The farmers are then joined by any town brothers they may have and they sit down together to evaluate the patrimonial property. No women participate in the deliberations. First, the men examine their land resources and make up sets of holdings of equal value. For example, if there are three farming brothers, virtually all the patrimonial land will be divided into three parcels; one parcel may have an extra *stremata* of vineyard as compared to the other two parcels, but that will make up for the fact that the second and third parcels consist of cotton lands which are slightly more fertile than those assigned to the first group of holdings. Once again, no brother knows which parcel of land will become his until after the drawing of the lots. Each man, therefore, has a strong incentive to see to it that the partition of the land holdings is as equitable as possible. If the mother of the men is still living, the brothers set apart several *stremata* of land which will become part of the share of whatever brother she elects to live with. This represents her dower right. Still other small parcels of land, on the order of five to ten *stremata,* are assigned outright to the brothers who are no longer farmers and do not live in the village. The token land is kept in their names, "so that they may remember their father," as one villager puts it. The conferees next turn their attention to their animal holdings and once again group these into parcels of equal value. Farm equipment and the outbuildings are treated in the same way.

Once the shares for each kind of property are decided upon, an enumeration of each share for each type of holding is written on a piece of paper and rolled up to resemble a cigarette. At that point, the women and children are called in and the time for drawing the lots has arrived. A neighbor or one of the children (never any of the adults in the family) is invited to draw the lots, first for the land, then for the farm animals, then for the equipment and outbuildings,and then for the houses. The moment is a tense one, for in spite of all efforts to equalize the shares some will be considered more desirable than others. The old house, for example, is not desired as much as one of the new houses, and the family that draws it may be disappointed. After the lots are drawn, the mother decides where she will stay. In one recent instance, she stayed with the brother who won the old house (he was not the eldest) because she felt more comfortable there. In another, the mother went with her younger son who had drawn a new house because his child was still small and her services as a baby-tender were needed.

When the whole procedure is completed, the personal effects of each brother and his wife and children are moved to the appropriate house, the furniture is distributed, and that night, for the first time, each family sleeps alone in its own establishment.

Descriptions given of the drawing of lots always convey the strong emotional involvement the participants have in the proceedings. The occasion heralds a change in the routines of life and in each family's attitude toward his property. The women tell of their tears and wails as they bid each other farewell before leaving to spend their first night in separate houses. They also describe their sensations of loneliness and strangeness under the new circumstances. The fact that the houses are almost always close together because they must be built on family-owned house sites in the village seems not to lessen the sense of dispersion as far as the women are concerned. The brothers continue as neighbors. They cooperate in agricultural activities much as unrelated neighbors in the village do: they borrow plows, draught animals, and other equipment from whoever owns it. In the meantime, the sisters-in-law may call on each other for help in the housework, they draw water from the same well, and their children visit freely in each other's houses. In other words, face-to-face associations continue at only a slightly diminished rate. But the villagers' conception of the separation as a drama of great significance is based on the change in point of view which accompanies it. Henceforth, each small family is free to develop its own resources as it wishes. The different personalities of the brothers and their wives manifest themselves in the way they administer their property and raise their children, and, most importantly each brother can now freely give his entire loyalty to his own wife and children and consider all new situations from the standpoint of how they will affect the smaller unit. He is now at liberty, in the village view, to make decisions advantageous to himself, even at the expense of his brothers. The burden of consideration for the welfare of others has been lifted and the brothers are now as free as the rest of the villagers to be rivals of each other. This is not to say that all kinship rights and obligations towards one's adult brothers and sisters and their children disappear, but rather that the emphasis of most intense concern shifts at the time of property division. Indeed, it is generally agreed that the longer harmonious relations among the brothers can be maintained, the better. As a matter of fact, it is just for the sake of keeping good relations that the villagers claim they draw lots for the patrimony. They explain that by so doing, they can manage the business of dividing the property *me aghapi* (with love). No brother can blame any other for the particular share he happened to draw.

The villagers take it for granted that neither impartiality nor altruism is possible in situations which involve one's own interests. They do not believe that anyone, even one's own brother, can act fairly out of principle. Therefore, they feel, some mechanism is required to enforce equity. The strength of their mistrust of the fairness of others is illustrated by a villager's response to a question as to why the mother was not invited into the deliberations. (Mothers who are still active normally have the respect of their adult sons and participate in other kinds of decisions.) The son explained that it was because she might show favoritism toward one of the sons. This explanation was given in spite of the fact that the lot system effectively makes it impossible for anyone to implement favoritism. It is chance that makes the decision as to who gets which share and when faced with the operation of uncontrollable forces of the universe, the Greek villagers say, *"Ti na kanume,"* "What can we do?" From their point of view, adverse decisions left to chance are easier to bear than decisions made by self-seeking humans. Therefore, in situations over which they could have control, they prefer, if possible, to rearrange the situation into one in which chance, or fate, if you will, makes the final decision.

In the late 1950's, the number of households in which any married son was still living with his father and mother was small, and there were none in which several married sons were living this way. The reasons for this are first, the decreasing number of sons who are remaining farmers; second, the age distribution of Vasilika's male population (relatively few men in the marriageable age group); and third, the increasing age for marriage even of farming sons. Five of Vasilika's elementary family households were the result of the separation of two sets of brothers in the early 1950's. In Vasilika, therefore, the existing composition of the households is a deceptive base for understanding the principles of organization of households in the village. The existent situation is one in which elementary family households predominate, but the mental construct which influences the formation of new households does not seem to have changed from the old expectation that several married farming brothers will live together. It remains as a latent principle, available for implementation whenever the circumstances warrant it.

Consequences of the Dowry System

The discussion of the dowry as a mechanism of inheritance for children of farmers who remain farmers may now be summarized. The dowry is part of a system in which children receive property through the parents of both their fathers and their mothers. Property from two sources merges in each generation and is redistributed in the next generation. Although patrilineally inherited lands (those passed from a father to his sons in each generation) have some continuity in space and have some continuity of ownership in the male line, such lands always constitute only one part of the total holdings of any particular elementary family. Therefore, in Vasilika and its vicinity, the pattern of land and money circulation through inheritance has two facets: one portion that is patrilineally inherited straight down the line of males; a second, distributed at marriage, that eventually circulates among unrelated elementary families. The system cannot be described as one in which women inherit from women, in spite of the legal residual control of a woman over her dower properties, because brothers have equal rights with their sisters to their mother's dower lands. In Vasilika, at least, there is neither an explicit nor an implicit pattern of giving daughters only dower property and sons only patrilineally inherited lands.

The combination of practices including the function of the dowry as inheritance, land as a major form of property, and village exogamy have some further consequences for the relation of property to groups of kinsmen in the Boeotian countryside. In spite of patrilocal residence and some patrilineally inherited land, the descendants of a male line are not associated with any particular landed estates. Since no man owns or farms exactly the same holdings as his father farmed before him, nor the same holdings his brothers have, and since he himself will expect to work different lands in different communities even in the course of his own adult life, the permanent association of certain estates with certain lineages is obstructed (Friedl 1959b). Moreover, since dowries move down the generations and not across to a man of one's own generation who might use the property to marry off one of his daughters, there is no economic advantage to brother-and-sister exchange marriages. This situation is congruent with both the Greek Orthodox Church's and the Civil Code's (Section 1357) prohibitions on marriages between sisters and brothers-in-law and between cousins to the third degree. This rule, as well as the bilateral reckoning of kin in Greece (Section 1356), prevents the transfer of property at marriage from resulting in either a series of equal exchanges between two sets of kin groups or in a regular pattern of circulation through several generations among particular sets of such groups. The control of property establishes social links between a man and his wife's relatives not only in the ways we have mentioned, but because his wife's parents and brothers and sisters have a legal and customary right to be consulted before the final alienation of dower property (Section 1418). These links last only one generation, however, so that in each generation a new network of relations between elementary families in the neighborhood develops, clustering around the management of dower properties. These matters are important because they reveal some of the economic and social structure of Vasilika and its neighborhood that is congruent with the type of relationships people, both kin and non-kin, have with each other (see Chapter 5).

One other situation occurs frequently enough in Vasilika to be worth mentioning. When a farmer has no sons to inherit his land and his house, but has a daughter, the father may acquire a man's assistance on the farm by importing a son-in-law. Such a man is called a *soghambros* in Vasilika; he is a husband who moves into his wife's household instead of vice-versa. The importation of a *soghambros* is also a solution to the problem of a young widow who has no grown sons to run the farm left by her husband and arranges a second marriage for herself with a man who is willing to work her first husband's holdings and her original dower lands. Since a *soghambros* is always a manager of, and the laborer on, property belonging to others and is expected to bring no property of his own with him, there is a slight social stigma attached to the status of Vasilika. The villagers say also that a *soghambros* is not "master in his own house." Certainly, the lot of a man who is not a master in his own house and comes as a stranger to a village where most of the other men have known each other all their lives is not a happy one. But a *soghambros* is not really dishonored by his position; the villagers, in this situation, as in so many others, recognize the practical necessities which brought about the arrangement and do not strongly condemn a man for making the best of his difficulties.

The dowry in Vasilika enters into the life of the villagers in other ways besides inheritance at marriage. It has long served as a means of upward social mobility for girls. Since, as we have seen, the marriage of a daughter is among the most important obligations of parents, the dowry comes into the consciousness of the villagers more often as a property requirement for marrying off their daughters than as a means of transmitting inheritance. When, in addition, the high value placed on upward social mobility is translated into an effort to find urban sons-in-law for one's daughters, the dowry emerges as a mechanism for increasing the social prestige of the family. Farmers are willing to give larger dowries in exchange for the great satisfaction they derive from having town sons-in-law. In Vasilika, the education of some sons has released land to add to the girls' dowries. Improved agricultural income has also enabled the farmers to give larger dowries. In the decade ending in 1959, every marriage of a Vasilika daughter whose father was in the upper half of the village's income range had been one with a man of respectable occupation who lived in a provincial town or in Athens. The husbands are tailors, small retail store-owners, or civil service workers. One young man is a photographer, another is a gymnasium professor who has become the principal of his gymnasium. In 1961, however, the son of a rather prosperous village farmer became attracted to a daughter of another Vasilika farmer with good land holdings. The young man asked his father to arrange the marriage for him, and, since all the conditions were entirely suitable, the young couple were engaged.

The trend in favor of town husbands prevails, however, among most of those who can afford it. Once a few girls had married urban men, the rivalry between village families led to greater efforts to secure town husbands for the others. Consequently, there has been an inflation in dowries which is alarming the villagers themselves. In the early 1950's, a *prika* worth $3,000 was enough for a town husband of no special prestige; by the late 1950's, the same kind of man was asking for one worth $4,500.

The inflation has had several consequences. Often the value of the dowry can no longer be limited to the share of the inheritance to which a girl is entitled. Farming sons are willing to give up some portion of their shares so that their sisters can "live well," as they put it. The brothers gain also from the added prestige and influence of the family. These in turn may make it possible for them to find a girl with a larger dowry than their property qualifications might warrant. A farmer so situated may make higher demands on the ground that his and his wife's children will have an urban aunt and uncle. The town sister might provide board for her nephews and nieces (girls are increasingly being sent to gymnasium) while they are in school and can also be expected to help them find jobs.

Another consequence of the dowry inflation is the increasingly late age of marriage for the village girls and the town men. It takes farmers longer to accumulate the larger amounts of cash for the dowry, and the prospective grooms longer to attain a position or income at least partially commensurate. Vasilika's girls who marry town men are usually between twenty-five and thirty. Those whose fathers have few land holdings, and consequently can offer only small dowries, have been marrying farmers from other villages or within Vasilika itself and have been in their early twenties at the time of the engagement.

Now let us consider the disposition of the dowry which goes with a girl marrying a town husband. First, if he accepts land as part of the dowry, he will of necessity have it worked by his wife's male relatives. In time, however, often by the end of the first decade of the marriage, the son-in-law may wish to expand his shop, or may wish to start building a house for himself or for his daughter's dowry, or may hear of a good investment opportunity. He will want money for these purposes, and so he begins, with his wife's consent and after consultation with her father, to arrange for the sale of dowry lands. Since the 1950's, prospective town grooms have been less willing to take land which they know they will eventually want to sell, and have been asking for cash or for a house in town. Anticipating this situation, several of Vasilika's farmers who have small daughters have begun to use their savings and even to sell a little land in order to build houses in Athens or in a provincial town so that by the time their daughters are ready to marry, the houses will provide the main portion of the dowry. Rents are high and earnings relatively low in cities so that houses are a good investment. However, since building materials must be bought, and contractors paid, in cash, the houses may take many years to build. The young couple may then move into the habitable shell, and the rest of the dwelling will be completed out of the farmer's then current income. This kind of dowry-on-the-installment-plan becomes part of the marriage contract. It is often a source not only of continuing long-term discussions between a farmer and his town son-in-law, but also a source of quarrels—what in Greece are called *fasaries*.

The rate of movement of farmers' daughters into the towns and cities has been accelerating in the last decade, but marriages to urban husbands are not a new phenomenon. Between 1930 and 1950, at least five of Vasilika's women married "into Athens."

This type of marriage, like those discussed above in which both bride and groom are members of farm families, accelerates land sales and exchanges. The network of association which develops between Vasilika's residents and their relatives in Athens and the towns, is, however, perhaps the most important consequence of the urban marriages of village women (Friedl 1959a). In addition to the economic reasons for continuing relationships, there are several customary patterns which increase the frequency of contacts between the two groups. Lonely village mothers are grateful for visits from their married daughters and their grandchildren, and the midsummer season not uncommonly finds city women with their children back in the village visiting their parents, often for as long as a month or two. A return to one's village for Easter, sometimes for most of the Holy Week as well, is a well-known pattern in Greece. *Paniyiri* in one's *patridha* (home village) is another occasion for visiting.

Journeys in the opposite direction also occur with some frequency. Village men and women, when ill, may enter hospitals in a town in which they have sons or daughters, or brothers or sisters. Village men visit their town brothers and bring their children; occasionally a child spends a summer with his town aunt or uncle. Visits to the village or to the town usually last several days. They are made possible by still another congruent pattern of Greek culture. Neither the villagers nor their town relatives seem to have any strong need for personal privacy. Visiting relatives are bedded down on pallets when there are not enough regular beds, and it is not considered either indecent or especially uncomfortable for one or even two families to sleep in the same room. It is through this intervisiting process that so many urban traits of culture are introduced to the villagers and, indeed, that some village patterns are conserved in urban areas.

An additional consequence of the town marriages of village girls is that rural wealth derived from land flows into the cities. This wealth is an addition to what the productivity of land normally contributes to urban centers in the form of food, taxes, and the export of rural produce. A portion of the farmer's profits, through the dowry, is being used, it would seem, directly to support a part of the urban population. When the dowries are invested in housing or in small commercial enterprises, many low-salaried employees, civil service workers, or economically marginal entrepreneurs find it possible to support themselves and their families in the town and cities. Without the aid of dower wealth, they might not be able to do so.

Attitudes Toward the Dowry System

Let us now turn from the nature and consequences of the dowry system to a renewed examination of the villagers' attitudes toward the dowry. They unquestionably think of the dowry as a burden. Raising daughters is called *vasana,* a task full of tribulations. The people of the village know that daughters are, in the long run, a net economic loss to the family. They strongly emphasize the burdens of having to give large dowries with daughters, and they rarely mention the size of the dowries sons will receive with their wives. When a girl is born to one of the more prosperous villagers, other men say with a certain suppressed glee, *"Tha plirosi,"* "He will pay," and they rub the fingers of the right hand against the thumb in a gesture of money payment. But the men who act this way have no corresponding phrase or gesture for what a son will bring in, and dowry inflation is always looked at from the standpoint of what must be paid out. Young prospective bridegrooms tend also to emphasize their roles as contributors to their sisters' dowries, rather than their roles as recipients of their bride's property.

In spite of their lamentations over the burdensomeness of the *prika,* the villagers regard it as a fixed feature of their lives. They invariably express puzzlement in conversations with Americans as to how any people can exist without it. Identifying the dowry with the trousseau, women ask how any girl can set up a household without one. They also ask how a dowerless woman can have any sense of economy, security, or support; how she can guard against the dangers of a shiftless husband.

The men say Greece is a poor country, and that therefore young couples need a double source of land or capital to assure the economic welfare of the new family. But at least of equal importance to the men is their feeling that their own self-respect depends upon the knowledge that they have provided for the future of their daughters—that they have enabled their daughters to "live well." When asked whether girls who did wage labor or who earned money from dressmaking used their earnings for their dowries, the villagers, men and women alike, looked shocked and displeased. They would say no, only fathers or brothers give dowries. Then they would explain that the girl gives her earnings to her father who uses it for the family's living expenses and may, if he wishes, return some to help in the collection of the trousseau, which, as we have seen, the men consider an insignificant part of the dowry. That the girls' earnings enabled the family to save other current income was a concept the villagers neither had a priori, nor understood when it was suggested to them. Neither did the villagers like the suggestion that by working in the fields the daughter of a farmer was contributing to the family's income and, therefore, indirectly to the savings accumulated for her dowry. As we have seen, in the context of farm management, they recognized the work of their women as contributing labor value, but in the context of the dowry, they did not see the situation this way.

The villagers act and talk as if they felt that it is the obligation of men to care for women, and that the obligation is largely fulfilled by the provision of a dowry for a daughter. The provision of the dowry is thus, in a sense, an outward manifestation of masculinity. By village custom, when a father dies or is incapacitated, a girl's brothers are considered responsible for marrying her off, and they are usually expected to fulfill this obligation before they themselves marry. This point of view does not correspond with the legal requirements. In the Civil Code (Section 1496) the mother is responsible for furnishing dowries for her daughters in the event of her husband's death or incapacity. The village attitude, however, I believe, is based partly on the feeling that most women are not capable of managing their estates and on the congruent custom of appointing male guardians to manage for them until their sons are grown, but more importantly on the basic notion that the provision of dowries is a male prerogative.

The emotional overtones accompanying the dowry system may be understood as a possible shift of emphasis from one kind of expression of male honor to another. Anthropologists who have worked in Greek Cypriot villages and in shepherd communities[3] report that the males in these settlements, almost all equally poor, based their sense of manly prestige not on wealth, but on the degree of honor they achieved by the protection of the chastity of their women. It would seem as if, in Boeotia, male honor depends not only on male protection of the chastity of women but also more explicitly and obviously on the provision by the men of adequate dowries for their women. The sense of satisfaction a man gets from dowering a daughter becomes more intense and compelling because the action is also an expression of his masculinity.

The shift of emphasis can be demonstrated in the village. Among the shepherds and landless or land-poor families in the village, girls marry earlier, with small dowries and trousseaus, and acquire correspondingly less prosperous husbands. The fathers and brothers involved, and the other villagers, comment on these unions by saying that early marriages are essential because otherwise the girls might run wild and disgrace the family. In other words, then, when economic means are limited, men can maintain their honor and self-respect only by protecting their women, and this becomes the paramount concern. The villagers seem to recognize that when there is no hope for even the modest degree of economic security and material well-being that the dowries of Vasilika's landowning farmers can provide, there is less impetus for the girl herself to remain virtuous or for her prospective suitors to respect her situation without the added emphasis on physical retaliation by her menfolk. However, flamboyant behavior and clandestine affairs could destroy the hope of a decent marriage for a girl whose father can provide a reasonable dowry. Or such actions might require an exorbitant dowry to overcome the effects of her bad reputation. For these girls, the rewards of waiting are great enough for them to be willing to postpone both

---

[3] John Peristiany and John Campbell, respectively.

marriage and affairs, so that there is less danger that they will allow themselves to be compromised and less need to claim male protection.

Yet, with all the difficulties and sacrifices required by the dowry and arranged marriage system in Vasilika, there have been very few young people who have "gone to the mountains," as the villagers phrase elopements of couples who have fallen in love. One or two such affairs seem to occur in each generation, at a time when the girl's male relatives are dead or not in the village; and among young people each of whose families have relatively few economic resources. The subsequent standard of living of the couples has been among the lowest in the village, and the men never fully recover from the stigma of such senseless behavior, from the villagers' view. Observable examples reinforce the villagers' argument that there is no hope for a decent life without a dowry, and reinforce their admonitions to their sons to wait for properly arranged marriages and not to be *trelos* (crazy) and run off to the mountains with a girl. The admonition gains force from the further observation that if the eloping young couples have little, their children will have still less. Any man who accepts a girl without a dowry is thought to be cheating his children of their rightful inheritance from their mother.

Yet, as we have had occasion to remark in other connections, the structure of marriage arrangements in Vasilika is not quite as rigid and as precise as the foregoing generalized description might imply. One Vasilika brother, in speaking of a sister who had become his responsibility after their father's death, remarked "Glory be to God (and he crossed himself) she met a man who liked her and was willing to take her with nothing but the *rukha* and what we had in the house." The unexpected can happen in Vasilika, and infant girls are still dandled with songs about how their beauty will some day attract a husband without a dowry.

Family and Kin Structure

The foregoing discussion of family activities and of the forms of property inheritance and circulation has by implication involved questions of family structure. By giving a newly married couple property of its own to manage, the dowry serves as a mechanism to separate the newly married couple structurally from either of their two sets of parents. This is true even when the farmers bring their brides back to their fathers' households. Such patrilocal residence produces the temporary situation of a functioning, cooperative, extended, patrilineal kin group, but one that is continually aware of its distinct component elementary families. We have said temporary because there is no contemplation that the several elementary family groups concerned will live out their lives in a joint, cooperative household.

The kinship terminology used in the village is congruent with the structure underlying the realities and expectations of the situation just described. Greek terms of reference for mother, father, grandfather, grandchildren, cousin, aunt, uncle, niece, and nephew are directly translatable into the English words, except that the linguistic forms vary for males and females, and that, in fact, the villagers refer to distinctions between first and second cousins more frequently than Americans do.[4] Like ours, the system is characterized by the distinctness of elementary family terms, the separation of generations, and the equal consideration of both father's and mother's line of descent in the terms for all consanguineal (blood) relatives. So far the Greek terms are also entirely congruent with the actual functioning distinctiveness of the elementary family and the existing bilateral descent in the country. There is special interest for us, however, in the Greek terms for affinal relatives (that is, relatives by marriage) which, in some instances, differ from those in English and are, in turn, congruent with the particular significance of marriage in Greek social structure.

Petheros (masculine) and *pethera* (feminine) are equivalent to English father-in-law and mother-in-law, but there is an additional, reciprocal Greek term which two sets of in-laws use in referring to each other: *simpetheros* and *simpethera.* In English these must be rendered as "my son's or daughter's father- or mother-in-law." The Greek terms, then, group together the parents of a husband and wife with a term of reference roughly translatable as "co-in-laws." The Greek word for son-in-law, *ghambros,* is also used to mean groom, and that for daughter-in-law, *nifi,* is also used for bride. Moreover, all the members of a man's elementary family, not only his parents, but also his brothers and sisters, all refer to his wife as their *nifi,* and all the members of a woman's elementary family refer to her husband as their *ghambros.* The terms *nifi* and *ghambros,* then, are not equivalent to any English kin terms, but must be translated as "that man or woman who has married a member of my elementary family." At least two generations, that of parents and their children, use the same terms to refer to people normally in the younger generation. In other words, the generational distinctiveness characteristic of terms for blood relatives is replaced by the status designation for a person who has married into an elementary family. This disregard of generation is not reciprocated, however, by the spouses of one's children or by one's brothers and sisters. As we have seen, mother and father of one's spouse are called *petharos* and *pethera;* now we can add that brothers and sister of one's spouse are referred to as *kunyadhos* and *kunyadha,* that is brother- and sister-in-law.

The status category of marriage into a particular elementary family appears again, however, in the existence of distinct terms by which men who have married two sisters refer to each other, *badzanakidhes,* and by which women who have married two brothers refer to each other, *sinifadhes.* Men who have married sisters and women who have married brothers have to deal with the same sets of in-laws and this constitutes a common bond which is signalized by the terms just given. Another way of saying this is that those women who are referred to as *nifi* by the same actual kin, also have a name for each other, *sinifadha,* and those men who are referred to as *ghambros* by the same actual kin, also have a name for each other, *badzanakis.*

---

[4] See Andromedas (1957) for a complete list of modern Greek kinship terms.

There is a reciprocal term equivalent in meaning, but not at all as technical in its connotation as the English word "spouse," whereby husbands and wives refer to each other: *sizighos*. Apart from this, there are no Greek words with the specific and exclusive significance of English "husband" and "wife." For husband, *andras* (man) is used; for wife, *yineka* (woman) or *kira* (lady).

The remaining terms in the Greek system that are related to marriage are those which refer reciprocally to a couple's marriage sponsor and the latter's spouse: *kumbaros* and *kumbara*. Moreover, the terms are extended on both sides to refer to the parents, brothers and sisters, and children of the original sponsors and their spouses when they marry.

Marriage sponsors may, but need not be chosen (and in the majority of instances in Vasilika are not chosen) from among one's biological kin. The term *kumbaros* is, however, properly considered part of the system of kinship terms because of a very weighty customary prohibition which the status of *kumbaros* imposes: the prohibition against marriage in the same degrees as those appropriate to blood relatives.

The same reciprocal terms, *kumbaros* and *kumbara*, with the same extensions to the kindred of each of the original parties and the same marriage prohibitions, are established between the parents of a child and his baptismal godparent (*nonos* or *nona*). Here again, parents may choose those with whom they wish to enter into this relationship, and individuals may or may not accept the request to sponsor a godchild (*vaftistikos* or *vaftistikya*).

Vasilika's inhabitants make use of the possibilities of the *kumbari* system in such a way as to parallel their search for affinal kin (in-laws). Just as the people of Vasilika select marriage partners for themselves and their children with an eye to the augmentation of material resources and social prestige, so they try to find *kumbari* whose wealth and position will be a source of potential help for themselves and their children. The similarity in functions of the two types of relationships is paralleled by their similarity in structural effects. Just as affinal connections preclude the possibility of marriage between any of the relatives of the two elementary families involved, so do *kumbari* connections. Moreover, since the people of the village apparently prefer to select *kumbari* from non-kin (they must do so with affinals), they succeed in augmenting their network of associations with what, from the standpoint of kin connections, is a random collection of elementary families and their bilateral kindred. Non-kin are more likely to be in other villages, and people of greater prestige in the towns and cities. Here again *kumbari* associations tend to lead out of the village, and there is frequently a disparity in the economic and social positions between villagers and their *kumbari*. On the one hand, some prosperous village farmers serve as godparents for shepherd families, and on the other, the aspiring farming families choose an urban merchant, or a professional man, as *kumbaros*. The parallel with relatives by marriage is most striking between *kumbari* through godparenthood, and the mutual obligations involved are larger in number, last longer, and are more likely to be fulfilled than those with marriage sponsors.

Still another parallel between in-laws and *kumbari* is that the individuals who fill these statuses are freely chosen, in contrast with consanguineal (blood) relatives who are, of course, automatically acquired by birth. Certainly this is a real distinction between the affinals and *kumbari,* on the one hand, and consanguineals on the other, but, in Vasilika at least, it is not a difference of preponderant functional importance. In practice, any significant relationships established even between consanguineal kin outside of the elementary family are voluntarily arranged, and this element of the situation is more important than is the fact that the pool of blood kin from whom a man or woman can make the choice is predetermined.

Let us summarize the situation this way: A man and his elementary family can normally provide all the personnel needed for the year-round functions on his farm. At peak periods the farmer hires the necessary additional labor. However, from time to time he may need temporary help. He may need an extra horse for plowing, or he may want to join with someone to fill a truck with grain for a trip to the mill or with cotton for a trip to the gin; or he may need an extra hand or two to string tobacco or to separate cotton from the pod, or he may want someone to help with irrigation, or he may wish to join with another family for the Easter feast. For both giving and receiving assistance of this kind, Vasilika's farmers seem to consider all the village's inhabitants, kin or non-kin, *kumbari* or non-*kumbari,* neighbor or non-neighbor, as almost equally suitable candidates. A farmer may choose one non-neighbor villager who has a good horse, and exchange plowing assistance with him, a next-door neighbor with whom he joins in sending grain to the mill, a village sister to help with tobacco stringing to whom he gives a bottle of wine or the like in return, and so on. Moreover, none of these arrangements is necessarily permanent; the personnel may vary from year to year and from season to season. Indeed, shifting relationships of this kind are more common than permanent ones. From our point of view, the significance lies in the fact that whether or not kin are involved, the type of association is the same.

There is one notable exception. No matter how valuable assistance might be, it is not sought after if the individuals capable of rendering it belong to a family with whom there is an acute, even if temporary, disagreement. For example, although one of the village girls was adept at giving penicillin injections, a woman from a family which was on bad terms with that of the girl preferred to leave the village for a week to live with a town relative who was also capable of giving the injections. The trip was inconvenient for the ill woman's family, and since she was not fond of her relative, the visit was actually distasteful to her. But neither of these considerations was compelling enough to have her choose what in her and her family's opinion was the worse alternative—to ask assistance from a village family with whom they were currently in acrimonious rivalry. Feuding of this kind can occur among kin as well as among neighbors.

Apart from the agricultural production cycle and other predominantly village-centered activities, Vasilika's farmers need help in arranging marriages, in educating their children, in finding employment, in dealing with government officials and with merchants to whom they sell their produce. They also want some urban associations simply for prestige, and to provide a place to stay if they visit towns and cities. For these extra-village purposes, a farmer is more likely first to survey his consanguineal kin, his affinals, and his *kumbari*. From among these, he may choose one of his first cousins with whom his son will board while he goes to the gymnasium, one of his sons-in-law who is a civil servant to help with tax problems, one of his *kumbari* to recommend a merchant, and so on. Again, the farmer chooses different individuals from among those potentially helpful to him by virtue of their statuses and need not ask any one person to help him in more than one way. Once more the relationships need not be permanent; if for any reason they prove unsatisfactory, a man shifts to another individual. Moreover, the farmer reciprocates these favors in various ways, for example, by taking his cousin's child for the summer, by offering hospitality to *kumbari* at festival times, or by getting information about village girls from among whom his urban connection may want to arrange a marriage. If a farmer can find no one among his group of consanguineal kin, his affinals, and his *kumbari* who is willing to enter into an agreement with him for these extra-village needs, he turns to his fellow villagers and neighbors and attempts to attach himself to their network of extra-village associations.

What Vasilika's farmers do not do is attempt to establish new and direct relationships with complete strangers, that is, persons or agencies outside the network of their own or their fellow villagers' extra-village associations.

In sum, then, outside of the elementary family, a Vasilika farmer expects to establish voluntary relationships with a number of different individuals from each of whom he expects the fulfillment of a limited set of obligations to himself, and toward each of whom he will fulfill an equivalent but usually not identical set of obligations. Each man is the center of a series of varied relationships in which those with whom he associates himself have no necessary connections with each other. He is the hub of a wheel that has no rim.

George Foster has called paired relationships of this kind "dyadic contracts" (Foster, 1961). He believes they will occur in societies in which the number of people to whom a man can have culturally defined obligations is so large that it is not possible for him to fulfill them all. Men and women, therefore, choose from among their many kin, godparents and the like, those with whom they will make dyadic contracts. The people and the situation in which the contract is enforced vary from time to time. Foster suggests that such sets of paired relationships deter the development of factional groups. The idea of the dyadic contract is an extraordinarily useful concept for understanding the relationships I have just described for Vasilika, and Foster's analysis illuminates the consequences of what I have just called a situation in which each man or woman is the hub of a rimless wheel.

In the next chapter, the quality of the human relations characteristic of the elementary family and of the other types of associations of the villagers will be discussed.

5

Human Relations[1]

Attitudes Toward Man and Nature

I F IT WERE NECESSARY to describe the nature of the villagers' feelings with
respect to each other and the world in one word, that word would be
"tension." Indeed, in the first chapter, the metaphor of Vasilika as a setting
for a series of family dramas was used. The metaphor has a special aptness because it hints at the essential quality of drama—tension created by some kind
of struggle. John Peristiany speaks of the agonistic quality of relationships
among the Cypriot villagers he knows—agonistic in the sense of the ancient
Greek word *agon* (match or struggle). This word is equally useful for Vasilika,
although the contests do not appear to have quite the intensity of those described for Cyprus. Nevertheless, in Vasilika, when one walks through the fields
and asks how the work is going, the common response is *"Palevume,"* "We are
wrestling." Such an answer is not a cliché in which the literal meaning is lost.
The villagers can amplify with further comments on their perpetual contest with
soil, weather, and machinery. Man does not always win, in their view, but he
is obligated to do his best and to use skill in the struggle. In contemporary
Vasilika, the skill involves knowledge of naturally efficient means, and anyone
who does not do his best in this sense is unintelligent and deserves to lose the
battle. Those who try may still fail, and then the villagers turn to fate or to
God's will as an explanation. But an appeal to fate or to God is never an excuse for neglecting actions which are humanly possible, and sometimes this is
overtly expressed. For example, one farmer, at a time of unseasonable drought,
remarked as he looked at his tobacco fields, "I won't make the sign of the cross,
I'll bring my pump over here and irrigate the field." His intent was not
blasphemous; he was not an irreligious man from the standpoint of village be-
liefs and practices. Rather, the farmer was expressing an explicit attitude in

---

[1] Lee (1953) is especially relevant to this chapter, and is strongly recommended
for further discussion.

village culture: man must use human means toward human ends, and this is his first obligation not only to himself but to God.

In Vasilika, the same tension—the sense of a contest, of struggle, of agony, of a kind of pushing and pulling—is also a feature of a large number of encounters with other human beings. In earlier discussions I referred to the economic rivalries among families in the village and to the efforts to keep family activities private to the point where a kind of espionage is practiced by all the villagers to uncover secrets. These contests we may now understand as one manifestation of the agonistic quality of many human relationships within the village. But seemingly perpetual battles require an occasional respite; the nervous vitality which they drain must be replenished. In Vasilika, some relationships within the family seem to contribute the respite and the energy to go on fighting the battles, whereas others appear to create the sense that perpetual struggle, principally outside the family, is a part of life. The family both starts the battle and also manufactures and distributes the weapons with which to fight it.

What is the ultimate aim of the battle, if I may continue the metaphor? It would seem that each man and woman seeks for identity, for a concept of self, and given the conditions of Greek village culture and its values, the search is carried on by pitting oneself against another, or against fate. One learns to know oneself primarily by contrast with others; and therefore the maintenance of some difference is a necessity. Contrasts, and the tension contrasts create, become expected and desired. Without change and variation the villagers lose their sense of life. But the need to engage in perpetual struggle is an emotional burden, especially because there must be some who lose in the contests. A man is not completely disgraced in the villagers' view, however, if he is bested in an encounter with another man, provided that he was willing to engage himself in the struggle in the first place and showed skill in his conduct of it. Just as agricultural failure is attributable to uncontrollable forces only if a man did his physical best, so failure in human relations is attributable to some other force only if a man has first made a creditable effort. It would seem that it is not the outcome but the continuing *aghonia* that gives a village man or woman the feeling that he is a functioning human being, that he has an identity, that he is alive. *"Perazmena, ksehazmena,"* "What is past is forgotten," the villagers say, and although they say so mostly in connection with unpleasantness, the saying is equally applicable to victories. For both victory and defeat are shortlived; a new area of battle constantly supersedes the old.

This struggle is not something which is entered into as a new pattern when men and women take on the responsibilities of a family, after a childhood spent without it. On the contrary, Vasilika's culture is one of those in which there is a continuity in the behavior and attitudes expected of children, adolescents, and adults. There are no sharp breaks; from their earliest days the upbringing of children plunges them into the role of agonist, and skills for functioning in this fashion are acquired in all stages of a child's development.

The villagers assume that intelligence and self-control are basic human qualities which differentiate men from animals. The villagers are in many ways committed humanists and assume that once these traits are developed each man will have the strength to face life and its *vasana* (trials and pains). Since they believe that children, by virtue of being human, have these traits inherently, the family's obligation lies in developing the traits to the point where the child, when he becomes an adult, can fend for himself. But until he is capable of independence in this regard he is especially vulnerable, and he is both subjected to the strains which parallel those he will have as an adult and also bolstered by the protective sheltering devices which supplement his own gradually developing abilities.

The process of caring for infants even during the first four months of their lives furnishes illustrations. Vasilika's infants are dressed in diapers and shirts and are than wrapped, with their legs straightened and their arms held down at their side, first in several blankets and then in swaddling bands. The result is a firm but not tight enclosure of the entire baby except for his neck and his head. Mothers explain that the swaddling is meant for the physical protection of the infant against cold and against objects which might hurt him. They also explain that only by restraint of the infant's random movements will he be able to grow straight legs and back.

But when one watches a mother wrap her infant and sees her make the sign of the cross three times with her fist over the baby before putting the swaddling bands on, and when one sees her make a spitting gesture three times toward the infant before placing on the swaddling band itself the blue bead that is supposed to protect against the evil eye, it becomes clear that the process of wrapping an infant is meant to provide a spiritually protective enclosure too.

Babies' helplessness makes them especially penetrable to the evil forces of human envy and under these circumstances external spiritual or even magical forces are believed to be necessary. Children up to adolescence are considered vulnerable, as we have seen, and this is expressed, among other ways, in the encouragement they get to participate in the formal religion of the village. They are brought to some church services as infants (except that both mother and infant are secluded at home and are specifically prohibited from entering the church for the first forty days after birth) and by the time they are three years old, children can stand quietly near an older member of their family through the entire two-hour Sunday liturgy. Parents encourage their children to join the young girls of the village in the Good Friday and Easter preparations as part of an expressed expectation that it will be good for their health. Fractious or complaining children, even when not ill, are thought to be suffering from the effects of the evil eye and may be taken to the priest for a special individual blessing to help dispel the influence.

As we have seen in connection with the blessing of a new house and its permanent sacred corner, God's protection and man's pleas for His grace continue as an accepted part of the life of the adults of the village. Here we may add briefly that this remains true even though adult men attend church services less frequently than women and ritual abstinences during Lent and similar formal requirements of the Greek Orthodox Church are not rigidly or systematically adhered to. Vasilika is a settlement in which there is some grumbling about, and some disregard of, the formal requirements of the Church as an institution; but God Himself, *"O papus apano,"* "the grandfather above," as He is sometimes affectionately called, is felt to be close, real, and not wholly inscrutable. He is an omnipresent force in the lives of men. Such phrases as *"Echi o theos,"* "God has (the wherewithal to provide)," fall easily from the villagers' lips as does the attribution to God, rather than to nature as an abstraction, of common physical phenomena: *"Vrechi o theos,"* "God is raining." The magical and spiritual protection which is available for children, then, continues to be available to adults but is considered less necessary and takes on a more formal religious guise.

Adult-Child Relationships

Let us return now to some of the strains that children are under. There are, of course, the ordinary physical hazards of life in a village like Vasilika. Children are kept from getting too close to the fires, to the oven, to other peoples' dogs; they are protected from the harsh effects of the weather. In addition, however, there are the hazards created by the behavior of other human beings. A woman suckling her infant, for example, may let the baby almost start to suck, then pull herself away, then let the child start again, then pull herself away. She may repeat these actions three or four times, talking and laughing as she does so, finally permitting the baby to suckle contentedly only after it has exhibited some discomfort by whimpering or squirming within its swaddling bands.

Such action is the beginning of a long series of similar teasing incidents in early childhood, sometimes connected with food, sometimes with other matters. A father of a two-year-old boy may call him over to have some of the sweet preserve that is being served to guests. The child runs eagerly to his father's knee. The father touches the spoonful of sweet to the child's mouth and as the boy opens his mouth to take the food, the father snatches the spoon away. He may repeat this several times until the child starts to cry. Then he lets the child eat, and hugs and pats him telling him he is a good boy.

In a different kind of situation, several boys of eighteen or nineteen encouraged the three-year-old brother of one of them to start a physical fight with his equally small cousin. The older boys shouted encouragement and made them intensify the pummelling of each other to the point where the children were knocking each other down and bruising themselves on the stones and rough earth of the yard. The little boys started to cry; the older boys laughed and then, still laughing, took the children into their arms and hugged and kissed them, calling them by endearing names. On one occasion, when a government agricultural extension agent was in the village injecting chickens against Newcastle's disease, a father lifted his little two-year-old son into the air, turned him upside down with the child's back facing the agent, and laughingly told the child that he would have the agent inject him just as if he were a chicken. The child started to cry, and after two or three minutes, his father righted the child and comforted him.

Sometimes adults use similar methods to discipline a child. On one occasion, a group of women were discussing the coming Easter festivities, and the two-year-old niece of one of them kept climbing on and off her aunt's lap. The child was told several times to sit still but ignored the request. Finally, her aunt laid the child on its back across her knees and laughingly told her they would kill her like the Easter lamb. The woman ran the edge of her hand over the child's throat to demonstrate the slitting of the lamb's throat. The others laughed and added vivid details. The child's eyes showed panic; she struggled up out of her aunt's lap and sat quietly on a stool for about fifteen minutes until they both left. We heard the aunt speaking gently and endearingly to the child as they departed.

As the foregoing examples indicate, when adults deliberately frighten children or even stimulate milder forms of distress, they do not abandon the child to his misery but try to relieve the anxiety by physical affection and soothing words. In spite of this, however, a three-year-old child will often try to hit a parent or elder brother or sister who is causing distress. He is laughed at for his futile efforts by those watching the scene. Four- and five-year-old children respond to the teasing by walking away or by maintaining stolid expressions. Once they do this, the severity and frequency of the teasing by elders decreases, and the pattern continues mostly among the children themselves in their relations with each other. Practical jokes continue on into adolescence. From the adults' point of view, the teasing is no longer amusing or valuable for discipline because the child has gained enough knowledge, enough intelligence to know that the process is a kind of game and has acquired the skill with which to handle his side of it. Mentally retarded individuals never learn, and they are baited and teased for the amusement of the watchers all their lives. From the child's point of view, the constant reassurance he receives after the pain may teach him that there is no real or permanent danger in the adult actions except that of ridicule, and that is what he learns to try to avoid.

Just as the teasing leads to a recognition that other people's actions and words should not be taken at face value, so does another common pattern of dealing with children—the pattern of deliberately lying to them. Usually, parents or older brothers and sisters lie to a child to get him to do what he does not want to do. For example, a three-year-old child may be asked to go into another room to fetch something. The child does not respond to several requests; his mother then tells him his father is in the other room and will give him candy if he goes. The child thinks he remembers that his father left for the fields early in the morning, and therefore is not likely to be in the next room; he makes a comment to this effect; his mother seriously reassures him that his father is really in the next room; he becomes uncertain and, finally, cautiously goes to the door, opens it slowly and looks inside. At this point his mother and anyone else around laugh at his look of chagrin.

Lying to children as a kind of palliative occurs in less dramatic ways as well. On one occasion, a mother was washing the legs of her two-year-old daughter. The child was standing on a table to be nearer the small water container hanging on the wall. When her mother finished, the girl did not want to come down off the table. She resisted, stamping her feet and calling for more water to play with. Her mother told her in a mild tone that there was no more water. This did not satisfy the child; she resisted further and finally the mother turned the spigot on and let her play with the water, of which there was quite a supply, for a few more minutes until the girl herself was ready to stop.

In both these instances the child easily detected the deceit of his elders. However, since there are occasions on which his father actually is in the next room and does give him candy, and other occasions when the water actually has run out, a child cannot know in advance when he is being deceived and when he is not. Inconsistency in the actions of elders results in a wariness in accepting or rejecting the statements of others, even within the family. Children may learn to love and respect their elders, but it is not required that they trust them completely.

Lying to children is one aspect of the general attitude toward truth and falsity characteristic of the village's adults. In the village the word for lies, *psemata,* is used much more freely, with less emotional intensity, and with a milder pejorative connotation than Americans use the English word. "Let's tell a few more lies and then go home," a man once remarked jovially near the end of a social evening. To accuse someone of mendacity is not the gross insult it is in the United States; it may be meant as a statement of fact in a situation in which, in village expectation, it would not be unusual for a person to attempt some deception. As in the training of children, some form of deception as a means of achieving a particular good is acceptable as a technique for conducting one's affairs in the village or with outsiders. Each man and woman expects to develop skills both in the art of guilefulness and in the art of detecting guilefulness in others. Vasilika's villagers are not humiliated because someone tries to deceive them; they become angry only if the deception succeeds. In other words, if a person is gullible enough to have been misled, he gets angry at the deceiver for having made a fool of him, and this results in accusations and counter-accusations. The standard phrase for deceptions means literally "He has made a laughing stock of me," *"Me yelase."* Older children who have learned to turn the tables on their parents and try to deceive them are admired even as they are scolded. Certainly any child who, in mild ways, learns to take advantage of a neighbor or another villager is privately approved of by his parents as *"ponyiros,"* "cleverly bad," although the neighbors use less ambivalent epithets.

The constant vigilance necessary to avert becoming a dupe is certainly one of the sources of tension in the conduct of human relations in the village. An American must not make the mistake of assuming, however, that these strains have the same effect on Vasilika's inhabitants that they would have on middle-class Americans whose training has included a stress on consistency and truthfulness. In Vasilika, the expectation of, and conditioning for, deceit does not eliminate the objective, realistic discomforts of living with somewhat unpredictable human beings, but the cultural expectation does seem to eliminate some of the intensity generated by the conflict.

The total situation does not result in an inability to predict the behavior of others to the point of chaos in human relationships, but rather in an expectation on the part of the villagers of a wide range of alternative actions and responses by others. There is uncertainty within set limits, but there is also an enjoyment of, and a taste for, the unpredictable. In a sense, when the villagers know each other so well that they can predict reactions with some precision, they are bored and look for other diversion.

Conversation and Argument

So far, teasing and deceptive acts have been stressed as elements in the contest of human relations. We may now turn to another type of weapon: conversation and argument. Students of Greek society and culture invariably mention the Greek's love of talk. The villagers of Vasilika are not different in this respect. Again, even infants become accustomed to a stream of conversation whenever others are around them, and they themselves are talked to and are assumed to make responses. When babies cry they are often said to be talking, *"Milai to moro,"* and *milai* is the standard word for talk. If a baby hiccoughs, they say it is talking to someone who is absent, such as a maternal grandmother in another village. By listening to the talk around him, and by participating in it, the young child learns the functions of speech. In the village, children may be told to be quiet when they interrupt adult conversation, but this occurs only when the elders do not want to be interrupted. Children are not silenced on any general principle that they should be seen and not heard.

A child in the village quickly learns that some kinds of conversations communicate information, that others are merely a verbal accompaniment to activities, and still others are a form of recreation and part of the contest in human relations. Inside their homes children hear discussions of plans for the day and speculations about the weather and about neighbors. This kind of talk is a form of fairly direct transfer of thought and information. The child also learns that many ordinary, apparently routine activities are carried on to the accompaniment of a stream of comment and advice and that only a small proportion of what is said genuinely influences the person to whom the advice is given. For example, if neighbors are visiting with a woman who is about to place some loaves of bread in the oven, a discussion ensues as to what design to use for the slits in the top of the loaf, as to whether the bread has risen sufficiently, and as to whether the oven is hot enough. The housewife may have been baking bread every week or so for twenty years, but the discussion could easily give an outsider the impression that she was a novice. Agricultural decisions, such as on just how to place a few corn plants in amongst the rows of cotton, are discussed anew each year. Even at a baptism in Vasilika, the ceremony is punctuated by comments as to whether the baptismal water is too hot or too cold and as to how to wrap the dripping baby after his total immersion. Guests call out remarks about the way the baby is being dressed; its bonnet strings, for example, are said to be too tight or too long, and so on.

Such comment and advice on recurrent, apparently routine activities serves simultaneously to express and to reinforce a particular point of view—the point of view that each event, no matter how often similar ones have occurred before, is essentially fresh and unique (Miller 1950:16). In a sense, the villagers impose variation and uncertainty on events which have no intrinsically adventurous elements. What, from the villager's standpoint, is the monotonous regularity of ordinary tasks is relieved by verbal exploration of the range of small variations possible. Even when people are alone they apparently prefer to change the time, or the place, or the order in which they perform recurring activities. For example, a woman who sifts flour and kneads dough for bread varies the time of day at which she starts the process, the part of the household in which she does these jobs (sometimes in the ground-floor room, sometimes in the storehouse, and in different corners of these rooms), and the extent to which she completes the sifting at one sitting. Some of these variations are dictated by external conditions such as weather or the time available from work in the fields; but others appear to be efforts simply to alleviate the felt boredom of routine activities. The feeling of security which many Americans derive from the regular performance of routine tasks seems unknown in Vasilika.

The stream of comment and advice associated with ordinary activities is very similar to the stream of orders and requests directed at children by their elders. Children learn that they are often not chastised for failing to respond immediately to a command such as "Katse kala," "Sit nicely," or "Be good." Moreover, they learn that specific commands to run errands or to stop playing in the mud will be repeated several times before a parent gets exasperated, and there will be other times at which the parent or older brother or sister is distracted by something else and will forget the command entirely. The tone of voice of the older person informs the child when an order is meant seriously, but, in the meantime, he responds to or ignores many orders about which his elders have a less firm conviction, and his reaction-depends upon his mood of the moment. The elders' words may even include threats that the child will "eat wood," that is, "be beaten" if he does not behave, and a parent may go so far as to threaten to kill a child who misbehaves. But even these threats do not elicit immediate response. (In fact, children are very rarely beaten. Physical coercion consists of an occasional slap on the back of the head, and children may be shoved, or pulled by the ear in one direction or another). It seems, then, that disobedience is not in and of itself considered a sign of disrespect to parents. In the villager's view, a child should listen to what his parents tell him because they are more intelligent, have better judgment, and have the child's welfare at heart. Very young children, the villagers believe, do not have sense enough to know this and so can scarcely be expected to respond without a bit of a push, and older children may be stubborn. Even pisma (stubbornness) is grudgingly admired in a child if he exercises it with moderation.

Children do, of course, run many errands and do respond to many orders given them. The point here is that the process has some of the quality of capriciousness we have seen in other contexts.

The capriciousness of human relationships is also understandable in the context of the meaning of village talk and conversation. The situation is one in which a child, following the example of adults, learns the appropriate verbal statements and responses but understands that much real communication occurs through tones of voice, bodily movements, and an estimate of the particular qualities of the particular event, rather than through words alone.

Talk in Vasilika, which literally aims at inducing direct action by others, also serves as a means of asserting a degree of equality in all human relationships. Just as children listen to, but need not accept, advice from parents, and parents receive comments and advice from their children that they may or may not accept, so people in higher prestige positions feel free to give advice and make suggestions to people in lower positions and vice versa. Social workers who occasionally visit the village have no hesitation in directly suggesting to a village woman that she take off her kerchief or that she have her teeth fixed. Conversely, the villagers do not hesitate to tell the social worker that she ought to eat more because she is too thin. Doctor and patient, waiter and customer, priest and parishioner, government official and taxpayer will, on some occasions, engage in the ritual of advice-giving. This pattern of relations cuts across the respect for expertness, for the skills of the specialist discussed in an earlier chapter. The right to a certain give-and-take underlies all relationships and serves to keep each situation unique and each relationship one of equality on at least some level. In agonistic situations, it is one means of reverting to an acceptance of common humanity.

Conversational skills are directly a part of the contests in two ways. First, skill in oratory and argument gives one an edge in the contests. The aim of the discussion usually is not to arrive at a rationally based conclusion or to exchange information, but to display skill at allusions, verbal quips, and niceties of expression. *Kuvenda* (conversation) provides men and women with an opportunity to boast of their own and their family's achievements and gives men a special opportunity to display their political knowledge and interest and to engage in political argument. Conversation of this kind has some of the quality of an arena in which each man displays himself as an individual and waits for an audience response. People talk at each other rather than with each other.

Second, talk enters into the agonistic relation when people try to elicit information from others by their questions and comments, and the others conceal as much as possible by their answers. If one gives a piece of news to another, and the receiver can say, *"To ematha,"* "I have already learned that," the receiver says it with a touch of pride and has scored a small point. The news of a serious accident to a member of one family will be divulged to other related families; unrelated families may pick up the information, but frequently do not pass it on, partially to avoid giving the original family undue prominence. The villagers acquire skill in extracting information by indirect means. One of their methods is to ask the same questions in different ways at different times, and an outsider is often struck by the persistence with which such questioning on the same issue is carried on over many months. Not to succeed in gathering a choice bit of knowledge is no disgrace—the villagers keep trying and every man stays on the alert to guard his secrets.

There are some kinds of verbal communication that are outside the realm of agonistic relationships and in a sense provide a respite from them. These are the ritual phrases, which constitute proper responses to frequently recurring common life situations.

Village manners require the use of a wide variety of greetings at meeting and at parting. In addition to these, there are a large number of appropriate set phrases for life crisis situations, large and small. For example, one says *"Kali eleftherya,"* "Good deliverance," to a pregnant woman, "May they live for you" to a parent showing you a picture of his children, "May it pass for you" to an ill person or to any member of his family, "To your health" to a person wearing new clothes, and so on. "Many years" is the wish expressed to everyone on saints' days. This list is far from complete, but illustrates the point that although the phrases are formulaic and are most often used without conscious awareness of their literal meanings, they are apotropaic in feeling. In other words, the villagers have a vague sense that the phrases, which are good wishes, may succeed in warding off evil. Certainly the formulas also serve as an immediate expression of the good intentions of the speaker toward another in a potentially stressful situation.

Transmission of Values

Some of the weapons used in agonistic relationships in the village and some of the processes by which children acquire the necessary skills to use them have been considered. It remains to complete the discussion of the kinds of values and attitudes inculcated in children and to show the relationship of all the foregoing to the question: Who are the actors in the contests of Vasilika, and what are the social alignments which form the structural base of these human relationships in the village?

If, as we have seen, obedience to elders is not a virtue which parents stress to regulate the behavior of children, and if affection is interspersed with ridicule so that children cannot depend completely on the parents' support, by what mechanism do the villagers' children acquire the prevailing standards of behavior? It has already been suggested that the villagers act as if they believed that human beings, by virtue of their humanity, have brains. It may now be added that they also believe that inherent in every child is a sense of integrity which, in English, is best translated as shame. Parents do not feel that they have to implant these traits in their children but expect to bring them to the surface and to put to use qualities which the child already has within himself.[2] Each child is believed to have rudimentary intelligence which will develop into rational

---

[2] I am indebted to Popie Mohring for this phrasing.

judgment, not through formal academic education, but by a natural flowering of common sense based on ordinary experience. Small children who get too near the fire or run too long in the sun are not scolded for disobedience but are excused on the grounds that they do not yet know any better. *"Dhen gzeri,"* they say, "He doesn't know." As children grow older, however, the same misbehavior is treated as a sign of unintelligence and accusations of stupidity may be flung at the child. *"Dhen echis myalo?,"* "Don't you have a brain?" they say.

The quality of shame which the villagers want to emphasize in their children is an inner sense of embarrassment at the thought of improperly revealing oneself—either the physical self (modesty) or the inner emotional self. The words for shame, which cluster about the term *endropi,* are used in at least three different contexts. When children refuse to talk to strangers, and smaller ones literally hide behind a parent, the elders say as an excuse, *"Drepete,"* "He is bashful." For young children to feel embarrassment at revealing themselves to strangers is proper in the villagers' view. As children grow older, girls are expected to be more modest than boys and shyness remains an excuse for females after it ceases to be one for males. The older women of the village, for example, find it difficult to join the men and visitors at a feast table; they prefer to eat in another room. They go into the *saloni* after their guests have finished eating and sit without speaking near the walls of the room. Villagers know that urban women do not have such reticences and they feel it necessary to make some excuse for their wives. *"Dreponde,"* they say, "They are ashamed," and although modesty as applied to a refusal to eat with one's guests is no longer fashionable, neither is it considered a disgrace to the husband or children.

A second use of the word for shame occurs when children show lack of self-control at stages in their development when it is already expected of them, *"Min drepese?"* "Aren't you ashamed?" is often a reaction of elders to a child who is less cleanly or orderly by village standards than he should be. Excessive running or shouting, physical fights with other children, loud and prolonged vituperation, enjoyment of food which borders on gluttony—these are the kinds of actions greeted with the suggestion that the child is exhibiting to the world too much of his inner needs. It is not the existence of the need that is considered bad, but rather the inability to control its expression. If he cannot exercise sufficient control, the child is not utilizing his sense of shame as is proper; he is making an unseemly exhibition of himself.

Although shame is considered an internal individual emotion, the process by which the villagers reveal his sense of shame to a child includes exaggerating and parading before others any evidence of possible shamelessness. That is, children are not merely asked *"Min drepese?"* but the action they should not have engaged in is often made much of and enlarged so that whatever inner discomfort is inculcated is reinforced by invoking the ridicule of outsiders. On one of our returns to the village for a brief stay, I visited one of my friends and casually asked where her five-year-old daughter was. Her mother answered that the child was probably hiding because she had been scolded for getting mud splattered on her dress. Some time later, as I was leaving, the mother caught sight of the little girl trying to hide herself on a narrow window ledge as she peaked out to catch a glimpse of the stranger. Instead of ignoring the child's discomfort, the mother went over to her saying, in a sarcastic tone, "Why don't you come out and show the lady your beautiful clean dress?" As we reached the little girl, the mother pulled at the child's dress and said, "See, Mrs. Ernestine, how clean she is?" And she said to the child, "Are you afraid to show yourself?" The child squirmed on the window ledge, held her fist to her mouth, and stared at me through these proceedings. She said nothing.

When older children misbehaved, parents sometimes threatened to tell the schoolteacher what they had done, with the implication that they would be both disgraced and punished.

Shame continues as a noticeable attribute of women throughout their lives. But as boys get older, an effort is made to enhance another component of their internal behavior, their love of honor (*filotimo*). A man expresses his masculinity by his love of honor; it is a necessary component of his self-esteem or *amour propre*. In Vasilika, a man gives expression to his *filotimo* by his fulfillment of his obligations to his family and especially to his women, by his ability to participate adequately in the daily give-and-take with other men, and by his knowledge of appropriate behavior toward visitors and guests of higher social position. A particular incident will illustrate: During a conversation with a bank manager in his town office, we were interrupted by a villager who wanted to talk to the manager. The manager told him kindly that he was busy; at a second interruption by the same man, the manager said to the villager, "Please leave us alone; don't you see I have guests here; have you no *filotimo?*" The man left immediately and did not return. The official had appealed to the man's own self-esteem to influence a change in his behavior. Moreover, if he had had to reprimand the man more fully before foreigners, the manager and the culprit would both have lacked *filotimo* as Greeks.

Self-esteem is also maintained in the village by a tendency to attribute failures to some outer conditions rather than to any personal inadequacy. If anything goes wrong, a man is most likely to say he did not have the proper equipment to do the job, or he says, *"Poz na ksero egho?"* "How was I to know?" or it is the fault of the government, or he has been deceived. Man's abilities, the villagers seem to believe, are always limited by the force of circumstances not entirely under his control—he has unexpected illnesses, he has more daughters than sons, rains come when crops need sun, governments establish regulations on matters in which he was not consulted; and since events such as these are part of the human condition, one or another of them is likely to be available for the explanation of any one man's shortcomings. *"O kakomiros,"* "the ill-fated one," the villagers may say of a man even in connection with routine mishaps. It is an epithet used often in the village and represents a compassion which does not derogate from the *filotimo* of the person referred to and counter-balances, to some extent, the frequent ridicule of the behavior of others.

Just as in Vasilika the avoidance of self-blame does not have the connotation of irresponsibility, so self-praise does not have the connotation of boasting. It is, rather, a necessary part of the maintenance of self-esteem. A host praises the food he is serving as he offers it to a guest; he talks of the accomplishments of his children; he tells of his exploits in the town; and usually he is the hero of his own tales. And since this must be done without giving too much information away, the stories have some of the vagueness of fantasy. As the examples show, however, self-praise is likely to occur with visitors as a part of the process of establishing a basis for a relationship. It is the relative lack of such opportunity in a small village, where everyone knows everyone else, that accounts for some of the complaints of the villagers about the monotony of village life. As I said at the beginning of the chapter, a desire for chances to contrast oneself with others, to enter into new situations, seems to be a strong impetus to action among the villagers and, in fact, an important source of the enjoyment of life. The warmth and generosity with which strangers are welcomed—the rightly famous Greek hospitality—may perhaps be understood partly in these terms.

The foregoing examples are undramatic in contrast with the violent defense of his *filotimo* required of a man whose daughter or sister has been dishonored. They fail to indicate the startling sacrifices of resources and energies that entire families have made in Greece to give hospitality to strangers or to protect fugitives of one kind or another, or the courage and daring with which a man may commit himself to a hazardous enterprise to express his honor and his sense of manhood. Such expressions of *filotimo* have been reported again and again from various regions of Greece.

The pattern of life in Vasilika, however, permits few opportunities for such dramatic incidents. A hazardous enterprise for our villagers cannot be a dangerous voyage in a strong sea, but must be, for example, a change from cotton to melon cultivation with an awareness of the risk involved. But the lack of extravagant situations should not obscure the underlying current of *amour propre* which characterizes the villagers—whether it be the sense of shame or of honor. For it exists and is always evident in the sensitivity, the tension, which characterizes human relationships and makes so many encounters a possible source of hurt and ill-feeling, as well as a possible source of triumph and satisfaction.

Noncompetitive Social Groupings

It now becomes possible to analyze the social field of the villager's agonistic relationships. Although some degree of competition in human relations is always present, even if only in a mild, bantering form, there are some social groupings in which agonistic relations play a minor part. The most significant of these is the elementary family. The unity of family goals and the dependence of each person on the others in the family for the maintenance of self-esteem limit the extent to which the home can be a battleground, although a child acquires from the behavior and attitudes of his parents, brothers, and sisters toward him the skills with which to battle. The elementary family is not only the most important economic unit in Vasilika, it is also a unit of *filotimo* and *dropi* (honor and shame). Each individual's actions reflect on his parents and only to a slightly lesser extent on his brothers and sisters and therefore contribute to the family's self-esteem. Since, as has been suggested, one expression of individual *filotimo* is not to admit one's own shortcomings, so a family will protect its members by overt support even when they engage in admittedly deviant behavior. An individual is told within the family circle that he is bringing disgrace on all its members, but he knows equally well that the family will protect him outside from as many of the consequences of his acts as possible. Families sacrifice much to send offending sons and daughters into other communities or to protect them in other ways. Children, in turn, speak well of their parents and tell of their accomplishments, even under circumstances in which the facts would not warrant such loyalty. The combat unit, for some occasions at least, is therefore the entire elementary family in its relationships with other families, and, indeed, with the rest of the world.

Congruent with this state of affairs is the fact that when the battle is not between families, the lines of antagonism are not drawn between age grades or sexes. The battle is not between the old and the young, or between men and women. It is rather old against other old, young against other young, men against other men, and women against other women.

Let us consider age groupings first. These are seen by the villagers roughly as pre-school children; school children up to twelve years old, at which time they have finished the elementary grades; adolescents, who are considered young until they marry; married adults; and finally elders, marked by the fact that their children are married. The divisions are not clearly defined and there is much overlapping, but to a certain extent each younger group treats the next older category of people with at least some of the deference with which all treat the elders; and each older group treats the next younger with some of the peremptoriness with which the elders are entitled to treat all others. Since the patterns of deference toward older men and the reciprocal nondeference are the standards for behavior among people of different social position, they shall be described here. Older men are always seated quickly and are not left standing under any circumstances. In the winter their seat is directly opposite the fireplace, while the women and children sit at right angles to the men. Older men are given the best chair the establishment affords; they are permitted to lean against the stalls in the front of the church while others usually may not do so. Young men do not smoke in front of their fathers; there is an avoidance of ribald conversation between the age groups. Older men in the village are addressed by courtesy titles such as *barba* (uncle) or, if considerably older than the speaker, as *papuli* (grandfather); and older men are always served first if there are no visitors present. Within the family, sons and daughters kiss the hands of their parents when they return after an absence. All children do this for respected elders who visit the village, while a large majority of the villagers on formal occasions greet the village priest in this fashion.

Elders in their relations with younger people address them by their given names and have the privilege of ordering them to run errands or to perform all kinds of small services. The tone in which older people order the younger is loud, often peremptory, and frequently is an exhortation to hurry. *"Glighora!, glighora!,"* "Fast!" said in a tone of command and dismissal, is perhaps the most telling expression of a superordinate person's relation to a subordinate. The reply is commonly *"Amesos!"* "Immediately!" or *"Eftasa!"* "I have arrived already!" These answers are forms only; younger children often set out at a run; others proceed at whatever pace pleases them at the moment. But the significance of these phrases for us is that *"glighora"* is never used by a younger person to an older one.

These expressions of deference, on the one hand, and of imperiousness, on the other, are outward signs of noncompeting relationships, because each age group and, by extension, each social status has rights, duties, and obligations, with one set of these shading gradually into the other with sufficient separation so that a complementary rather than a competing relationship predominates. Preschool children are expected to learn what elders in all categories teach them and otherwise have few responsibilities. School children, both boys and girls, take on the burdens of life, because their success in school is a matter of vital concern to themselves and their families. During school holidays school children from ages seven to twelve are expected to help with farm work. When they have finished elementary school the children consider themselves adult (they said so in a set of essays we asked them to write on what they wanted to do when they were grown) and expect to contribute to the welfare of their families, either by taking on more and more responsibilities on the farm, or by apprenticeships to trades. This is the period in which comradeship is most possible. Each boy tends to have one other boy as a friend and companion. They visit festivals together, go to the coffeehouse, and play cards together. Girls have less opportunity for free movement and are more likely to sit and work with their age companions in neighborhood work groups. Whatever work these older boys and girls do on the farm is supervised by their elders, and the supervision is accepted. Nevertheless, as explained already, each person has the right to contribute his suggestions and advice, and although a father or older man has the right to make the final decision, he rarely chooses one that will anger his younger assistants.

Here again, the young people work in a complementary relation with other members of the family; their goals are the same as those of their elders—to do well so that a good marriage can eventually be arranged—and the various means by which to achieve these goals are not in dispute. In spite of the rapid and accelerating technological and material changes in the village since the end of World War I, these changes have not led to conflicts between the generations. As earlier chapters have indicated, old people are basically no less "progressive" than their juniors; young and old continue to agree on the goals and on the means to achieve them as they change, and each has his part to play in the achievement of the approved ends. The grandparent generation joins with the rest.

Once the young people have married, they either continue as farmers in the household of their parents and gradually take over more of the supervision of the work, or work separately as a new elementary family. Therefore, to return to our original remark, the agonistic quality is not characteristic of relations between the generations.

The kind of competition we have been describing as agonistic does not prevail between the sexes in Vasilika. Men and women are considered far too different from each other for that. In the farming life of the village, men and women work, for the most part, at different tasks inside the households and in the fields. Men go to the coffeehouses alone and talk politics among themselves, women do neither; men do not discuss politics with women. In 1956, at a time the men of the village were agitated over the Cyprus issue (as was the entire Greek nation), a woman announced to a group of other women one morning that the English had hanged two young terrorists on Cyprus. Only one other woman in the group of five knew what she meant, and one of the group had so little knowledge that she asked, "What is Cyprus?"

The strength of the conceptual differentiation of men and women in the village may be judged from the expectation that the women will give men the kind of deference the young give the old. Men assign to women, and women accept for themselves, some other attributes of the young: modesty; greater emotionality and sensibility and, therefore, a longer continuing struggle for self-control; less rationality; and a greater vulnerability, which necessitates assistance from their menfolk and from the supernatural.

Americans are struck by the separateness of the preoccupations and activities of men and women in Vasilika. Men and women meet only with respect to their joint family obligations—the responsibilities of procreation and of supporting their children. Among the villagers there is even an atmosphere of covert mutual dislike between the sexes. Men express contempt for what interests women and vice versa. The spheres of activity in which men and women support each other have to do with the honor of the family and constitute a division of labor based on sex but with a curiously sexless quality. There is no mutuality between the sexes in the village when the needs of masculinity or the needs of femininity are involved. The women have little patience with, and may even fear, male extravagance in efforts to maintain *filotimo;* men have little patience with emotional crises in females.

It is difficult to write of these characteristic attitudes without creating a distorted picture of women as an inferior sex and of males and females at war with each other. The male-centeredness of Greek village society is undeniable; but neither are women wholly without rights. For example, the avoidance of places where men gather is a form of modesty, as I have suggested, and not an admission of inferiority. Women have their own conversational groups of working neighbors which men do not join. In addition, the economic functions of the dowry and the residual control women maintain over it gives them considerable voice in the decisions made within the family.

Finally, the residual equality of a common humanity which appears in the reciprocal comments and suggestions between people in superordinate and subordinate positions—at least in the village—again mitigates the severity of the relationship betwen the sexes. Nor should we leave the subject without mention of the accommodation many couples make to their marriages or of the frequent development of mutual affection between husband and wife who find themselves compatible as individuals once they have worked together to raise a family. What I wish to explain here is that mutual respect and affection between a married couple can develop in Vasilika, but that in order for it to do so, the husband and wife must overcome overt cultural attitudes of deference and covert attitudes of sexual mistrust as well as what are undoubtedly unconscious conflicts about sexuality.

If there is tension between men and women in Vasilika, why is it possible to say that agonistic relationships do not exist between them? It is because the cultural differentiation and separation of the sexes makes them unequal and therefore not in a position for the direct, overt competition of which agonistic relations consist. The maintenance of this differentiation in the qualities and characteristics of women acts as a foil for the men—once again the contrast gives meaning to the self. For women, also, the contrast serves as a means of self-identification.

If age and sex are not the lines along which agonistic relations occur in Vasilika, then what is the structure of these relationships? Essentially, agonistic relations occur among those who, from the standpoint of village culture, are both separate and equal, and among men of the same age categories and women of the same age categories who are not members of the same elementary family and are in the same or adjacent social positions. This includes brothers in their relationships with each other and sisters in theirs, once these have married and have elementary families of their own. I have already suggested that brothers are rivals, and sisters also compete for the greater success of their husbands and children. Within the village, people who are not related to each other compete also, as do the people of Vasilika with the inhabitants of neighboring villages.

It is now possible to understand why, from the villagers' point of view, their cooperative arrangements with each other and with their urban connections tend to be impermanent (see the end of Chapter 4). Each request for help and each response to the request becomes part of the competitive struggle. The value of what is given and what is received must be judged at each encounter, and the potentialities for imbalance are always present and are frequently realized.

The alignments of kin and non-kin which lead outside the village and the quality of human relationships, both among the people of Vasilika and with those outside the village, have bearing on the nature of the village as a solidary community. This matter is the subject of the last chapter.

6

The Village: As a Community

The Village Government

IN THE FIRST CHAPTER the village was described as a setting for the life of families, which are the most significant social groups in the settlement. It now becomes possible to consider the functions of the village itself as an entity in its own right. First, the formal organization of village-wide activities and responsibilities will be discussed, and second, the attitudes of the inhabitants toward Vasilika in contrast with their attitudes toward the family and the nation.

The Greek government classifies Vasilika as a *kinotis* for administrative purposes despite its small population. A *kinotis* is legally a populated center with at least 300 inhabitants and a school, and constitutes one of the four kinds of administrative subdivisions in each of the nomes (provinces) of Greece.

The formal governmental activities of the *kinotis* are the responsibility of a locally elected president and council. A community the size of Vasilika is entitled to a council of five members elected for a four-year term. Voting must be done along party lines; and voters select five names from among those listed by the party of their choice. Vasilika had only two political parties in its local elections in 1956. Under the system of proportional representation then operating, the four men with the most votes from the party which itself had the majority of votes were elected to the council. The fifth member should have been the man with the most votes in the minority party. At the last Vasilika election, however, the man in this position preferred not to act as a minority representative and the second man on the list became the council member. The five representatives then elect a president and a vice-president from among their number, usually for two-year terms. The council and community are served by an additional official, the secretary of the *kinotis*. The secretary is not elected and has no vote on the council. He is appointed by the nomarch (governor) of the province upon nomination from the village council. His salary varies with the income of the community. The secretary tends to remain in office for many years, thereby becoming the equivalent of a permanent civil servant.

The president is held responsible for the completion of the tasks assigned to him and to his council. These include registration of births and deaths, a census of males every five years, the physical maintenance of the roads and public wells in the village, the preparation of the community tax rolls, and the preparation of an annual village budget.

In a community the size of Vasilika the maintenance of vital statistics is not an onerous task, since births, deaths, and the age and sex distribution of the population are matters of common knowledge. The maintenance of village property is a more complicated matter. Funds for materials are available in the village's account, which is held by the treasury at Amphiklia. The community may not draw on its account without the approval of the nomarch. Therefore, any public works program in the village is first formulated by the council and then sent for final approval to the nomarch's office. Village males who are more than fifteen years old are responsible for providing labor for road building and for minor repairs of village property. They may either give a certain number of days a year to work on such public projects or fulfill the obligation by furnishing money for a substitute. There is no effective practical way of enforcing adherence to the commitment. The state of the village roads and wells depends, therefore, on whether the village men are willing to work together to create a village asset.

In the course of our 1955–1956 stay at Vasilika a special impetus for road repairs presented itself. The council had requested that one bus a day traveling between Kifisokhori and Levadhia be rerouted so as to pass through the village. The nomarch had indicated that he would approve the change if the village road was repaired, and he authorized the necessary materials. One day in March, truckloads of earth were brought into the village and about one quarter of the adult male population shoveled the loose earth into the main ruts on the village road. The road was superficially improved thereby, and a month or so later a bus was routed through the village. The poor drainage from one of the wells was not corrected, however, so that the regular spillage from the well quickly restored the old puddles in the road.

The men and boys who worked on the road project lacked their customary vigor. Indeed, the majority of the male population of the village claimed to have work to do in the fields that day and did not join in the road work at all. There was much joking, teasing, and clowning while the work was going on, and the efforts of two of the older men to convince the group to set to work with a will were unavailing. The attitude of the road workers requires explanation because all the villagers were agreed on the importance of the new bus route and they actively dislike mud. The muddiness of the village road in winter and early spring was a particular subject for comment and several times evoked the question, "Do you have mud in America, too?" An Athenian who visited the village in late spring was critical of the villagers because their *aghora* was unpaved. "Don't you have a lot of mud all winter?" she asked. "Oh no, we don't have any mud in winter. Very little," was the response from one of the villagers. He would not even admit to so unsightly a condition.

The reluctance of the villagers to work on the road seems to result not from a lack of motivation but rather from a more compelling distaste for manual labor, and especially for such work when it does not directly or immediately benefit each man's own family. Several years later when a new school was built, some of the parents of the school children helped with parts of the construction. The other villagers did not.

The preparation of the community tax rolls is an important responsibility of the village council. Since taxes are based on land tenure, on produce, and on livestock ownership, the council must prepare lists of people who own land within the boundaries of the *kinotis*. The lists include for each person information on the number of *stremata* in each parcel of land he owns, on the kind of crop raised on each parcel, and on the quality of the land. Lists of the number of horses, mules, sheep, and goats owned by each villager are also compiled. Donkeys and chickens are not taxed and no listing is made of them. The tax is calculated for each item and the completed tax rolls are posted. A villager may feel that he has been unfairly treated, that, for example, the quality of his vineyard has been overestimated or that he has fewer sheep than the number listed. In such a case he can request a revision from the council. His request is usually granted and that settles the matter. If he is not satisfied, he may ask for a hearing before a grievance committee, the members of which are proposed by the council from among the villagers. Any decision of the committee is subject to the veto of the nomarch. In Vasilika disputes over tax rolls are said not to occur, and no grievance committee has been established for many years. There had been a dispute with Parori in the 1930's over the boundaries of the two communities. Since each *kinotis* receives taxes from the land within its boundaries the question of where one *kinotis* begins and the other ends is of considerable importance. The argument between the two villages was finally settled in the courts.

In connection with the preparation of tax rolls, the president has some power over the shepherds living in the community. Anyone classified as a nonresident of Vasilika must pay double the rate for pasturing his animals there. If no permission has been granted, he must pay triple the rate for residents. The question of when and if the new settlers in Vasilika—the shepherds, who had been living there since 1950—would be considered residents of Vasilika, that is, full-fledged citizens of the *kinotis,* was of significance both to the village and to the shepherds. They were finally granted this privilege in 1959.

The actual process of preparing the tax rolls consists of a series of agreements among the villagers, including their council members, as to what amount of property they will declare. In consequence, the tax rolls do not necessarily represent an accurate and complete accounting of property ownership in the *kinotis*. Farmers often try to hide some of their holdings and keep some of their transactions quiet. For example, in order to pay less in taxes on the value of dowries, the records may show the transfer of a smaller parcel of land to the groom than the one privately agreed on and later privately carried out. Records are probably being kept more accurately now, since credit from the Agricultural Bank is based on land holdings, and proof of ownership must be given to the bank.

The village council also has initial jurisdiction over monies which are not derived from the taxes already mentioned. There is a levy amounting to two percent a year of the value of the cotton and wheat produced by each farmer, three percent of the value of any inheritance, and three percent of the value of money and property given as a dowry for any village girl. The proceeds of these taxes are deposited in the village account in Amphiklia. A tax on tobacco production is paid to the national government. The amount collected from the tobacco tax is redistributed to all communities in Greece on a per capita basis for schools, roads, and the like. Tobacco-growing villages like Vasilika receive an additional sum in proportion to the quantity of tobacco produced in the community.

Initial jurisdiction in the disposal of all monies belonging to the *kinotis* consists in the preparation of the village budget by the council. The task is done under the close supervision of the nomarch's office. Printed forms for village budgets are available at stationery stores and must be purchased and used. The form includes a list of items for which the community may be expected to spend its money and another list of items from which income is derived. It is the secretary's work actually to fill in the form in quadruplicate. He does so at a meeting of village secretaries called by the nomarch and held in Levadhia. The forms are then checked by the nomarch's office and some changes may be imposed. The expenses listed on the form include the secretary's salary, the salaries of the two village policemen, the salary of an assistant treasurer in Amphiklia, whatever is due the tax collector (who seemed in 1956 to be getting six percent of the amount collected), rent to the church for office space, several newspapers brought by train from Athens each day, books for the school (but not for individual students), road repairs, and the like. The completed document becomes, in fact, a theoretical model for appropriate village income and expenditure rather than a reasonable estimate of future financial transactions. Some of the income actually will be deposited in the account of the village and some of the expenditures will be made, but most will not, and even those transactions that do occur may not be made in the sums designated in the budget.

Let us consider income first. The collection of taxes from the farmers is not carried out regularly. When no collector comes to the village, the farmers are supposed to go to Amphiklia to pay their taxes, but few do so. During our stay in the village, a new collector came to Vasilika and sat in the *aghora* for an entire day accepting money from the farmers. They paid only part of their previous year's assessment, and so remained a year in arrears. The interest charge on late tax payments is only sporadically collected from the farmers. Just as the collection of monies is irregular, so is the payment of salaries and the expenditure of other funds. For example, the secretary at one point had not received his monthly salary of 350 drachmas for several months. The use of monies for other purposes depends on the interest of the villagers in village projects, and for the most part such interest is lacking. The village governing body and the secretary fulfill the formal responsibilities placed upon them by the national government, but do not seem to feel that the forms must reflect reality.

It is clear from the foregoing that in the formal political organization of Greece the village council has little power even over affairs for which it has some responsibility. The collection of its monies is undertaken by the central government's financial officers directed from Amphiklia, and the expenditure of its monies is supervised and controlled by the officers of the *nomarchia* centered in Levadhia. Moreover, the council has neither responsibility nor power over other village-wide activities. Law enforcement and the operation of the village school and of the village churches are administered separately both from the council and each from the others. Before turning to these activities, some mention of the council's role in Vasilika apart from the formal expectations is appropriate.

It is indicative of the village attitude toward the council, in contrast with that toward the president, that at no time during our stay in the village was any man pointed out to us as having the status of council member or as having had it in the past. When, accompanied by several villagers, we visited the former schoolteacher of Vasilika, he asked us who was currently the president but did not ask about the council members. The president has an important role to play in the minds of the villagers. He is expected to act as liaison between them and other governmental units and to further the interests of Vasilika in whatever situations may develop. For example, there was some criticism of the president for not arranging more rapidly for the bus to come through the village. In early April 1956, an unexpected and heavy rain flooded the fields and threatened to destroy the wheat if the waters did not drain off quickly. Most of the villagers (not all, however) were agitated, and in the early morning groups of men climbed the hill and looked out over the fields shaking their heads and lamenting, "*Katastrofes!*" "Catastrophy!" Then came the discussion of why the fields were not draining properly. All day, in the coffeehouse, the men inveighed against the English company who had owned the former Lake Copais land for setting up a drainage system that did not go beyond those lands; against the Greeks who took over the company for continuing a system that, the men insisted, not only did not drain the lands of Vasilika, but even made it subject to flooding; against the government for not having built a proposed dam that would have protected the region; and against the village president for not immediately calling on the nomarch's engineers to suggest remedies for the present situation. For days after, there were rumors that the nomarch's technical staff would meet with the president and councils of Parori and Vasilika to arrange a public works program of low dams to protect the area from possible future disasters from the same cause. The meeting never took place. Some villagers blamed the situation on the unwillingness of the farmers to work together to build their own small dams. One man had earlier tried to protect his own fields by building low earthen dikes around them, but his work was wasted because the surrounding fields were not so protected. The morning after the storm some of the men had quickly built up a two-foot dam at an obviously vulnerable spot near the cemetery. But a villager pointed out that if the water had risen just a little further, the placement of the dam would have made the situation worse rather than better. There was no more rain; the waters gradually receded; each man watched for his own fields to dry out. Those who were left with one or two small plots that were so badly flooded as to be useless for planting that season accepted the fact with resignation. The agitation died down after several days and the matter was not mentioned again.

Let us return now to the other officials and organizations that have responsibilities concerning the village as a whole. Law enforcement in Vasilika is in the hands of two *aghrofilakes* (rural policemen). They are appointed by the nomarch and are responsible for preventing and detecting animal trespass in the fields and thefts of produce as well as of personal property. They also watch sales of cotton and tobacco and can therefore furnish information of value for estimating produce taxes. The village police are sometimes called in to deal with disorderly conduct or with any physical violence which threatens to become serious. The *aghrofilakes* wear grey uniforms with green trim and are easily distinguished from the other villagers. Vasilika's police used to be *kseni* (strangers) who came from two different neighboring villages, but in 1961 the men were natives of the village who were relatives of the then current president.

There are two other semigovernmental village-wide organizations: the agricultural cooperative credit society, and the welfare committee. The villagers elect a president of the credit society, whose signature is necessary on almost all requests for credit, since the Agricultural Bank works in conjunction with the cooperative. The village priest, the president of the council, and the president of the agricultural credit society constitute the welfare committee. They attest to the financial need of a villager who wishes to avail himself of free government welfare services. In most cases, however, the village families who occasionally need help receive irregular gifts of food and clothing from other village families, and their plight is not considered a matter for joint village action. When several cartons of surplus American butter, cheese, and powdered milk reached the village, it was the priest who distributed the goods. On that occasion, the daughter of one of the recipients brought some butter (which the villagers usually do not use in cooking or baking) to a neighbor's daughter, who contributed eggs, flour, and sugar. The two girls spent a busy afternoon mixing a cake according to a half-remembered recipe given them by an extension worker some years before. The cake was not a success by any standards for such confections, but the girls were satisfied because they had produced a European-style sweet.

The Village School

The village school is supervised and controlled by the Ministry of Education in Athens. The teacher is appointed by the ministry, which also prescribes the curriculum. In Vasilika, in 1955–1956, the school had thirty pupils distributed unevenly among the six grades. The first grade had the largest number of children because its ranks were augmented by the children of the shepherds, some of whom had had no previous schooling and were assigned to the first grade regardless of age. A man originally from the Peloponnesus taught the children. He had married a woman from Parori, who was herself one of the school teachers in that village, and whose father had been a school official. They lived in Parori and the school teacher walked back and forth each day. He is a man much interested in improving the standard of living in the region by increased arboriculture, by the maintenance of kitchen gardens, and by the raising of rabbits, pigeons, and other fowl for food. The teacher covers the standard academic curriculum—reading, writing, arithmetic, geography, history (with emphasis on the ancient and modern history of Greece), and Greek language, as well as some religion. For the most part, he uses the traditional methods of rote learnng, but occasionally he includes some material on farm practices in his lessons, and tries different teaching techniques. On one occasion he supplemented the geography lesson by having the children make in the schoolyard an earth model of the topography of the Peloponnesus. He had them bring small samples of each of the products grown in the different regions of that part of Greece to place on the appropriate spot on the model.

In 1959, there was much favorable comment in the village because the schoolteacher had succeeded in having the new school built in just four months —a very short period for construction work of that kind in the region. But the schoolteacher is always partly an outsider for Vasilika because he neither comes from nor lives in the village.

The school and its teacher are a focus of interest for all village families with school-age children. Not only does the school have its obvious educational functions, but the teacher is a supplementary authority with whom parents can threaten their children, and the success of their children in school is a source of great pride to the parents.

On two occasions in the course of the year the school becomes a focus of interest for the entire village. The first of these is *Ochi* Day (the 28th of October), when the school children wear the old rural costumes and declaim patriotic poems to commemorate the day in 1940 when the Greeks said "No!" to the Italian ultimatum and started to repell the Italian invasion. This is a national holiday, and the village president and the priest participate. On the *Ochi* Day that we witnessed, however, the audience for the ceremonies was small because the adults were out in the fields picking cotton.

The second occasion is the more important one, *Evangelizmos,* the Feast of the Annunciation on the 25th of March. That is the official date on which, in 1821, the start of the revolution against the Turks was proclaimed by a bishop, and it is celebrated in Vasilika by children's recitations at the church services and by a school dramatic performance afterwards. The teacher selects the playlets, which usually include several that are re-enactments of the partly legendary incidents of the revolution. After the children have performed, the young men of the village present one or two mildly bawdy skits, which derive their humor partly from the antics of the boys who are assigned female roles and wear women's clothes. After the plays, the children, still in costume, perform some of the folk dances of the region, accompanying themselves with songs. *Evangelizmos* is one of the few times in the course of the year when virtually the entire village appears at an event. Villagers of all ages and both sexes come to watch the plays, and together concentrate their attention for over an hour on exactly the same activity.

The Village Church

The affairs of the church in Vasilika are administered by the priest with the aid of a committee of four men. Committee members are selected for three-year terms by the bishop from a list sent by the priest. One of the members of the committee is the treasurer for the church. He makes the collections at services and generally supervises the church's funds. In Vasilika income for the church is derived from the Sunday collections, the sale of offerings of wheat and olive oil made on special feast days, the sale of candles, rent on church property such as the old school building and the community office (both of these buildings were put up by the church as an investment), and the sale of produce from some twenty church-owned *stremata*. The priest is now given a small salary by the national government, but one-quarter of the church's income must be returned to the national treasury as a partial contribution of the community to the priest's salary. The other expenses of the church include the salaries (eighty drachmas a month) paid to each of the chanters and to the sexton. In Vasilika, the latter office is held by a sixty-year-old woman who is often assisted in her duties by her grandchildren. The physical maintenance of the buildings is also a responsibility of the church committee, and in 1959 they arranged for an extensive renovation of the main church.

The description just given is that of the formal organization of church affairs. In Vasilika the priest himself has more than his share of influence on all decisions and, indeed, it was said that one of the committee members in 1956 never went to any meetings of the church committee (they are said to be held about four times a year). The priest is a native of Vasilika, in his sixties. He is a strong, vigorous, and imposing figure, somewhat taller than the average villager and with a personality, temper, and voice to match. As he chants the liturgy the priest's deep voice fills the church, so that the elegant cadences of the Greek Orthodox mass gain added beauty. Because the priest and his sons have arranged his patrimony well, the priest as a private landowner is one of the more prosperous men in the village and for that reason, as well as for his personal qualities, he commands considerable respect.

Under the leadership of the priest, church affairs can, on rare occasions, involve the entire male population of the village. At about one o'clock on a rainy Sunday afternoon in the fall of 1955, the church bell rang. The men and the boys of the village streamed down the hill into the *aghora*. There they stood in the heavy rain as the priest, in his flowing black robes, as usual, and holding the only umbrella in the gathering over himself, began an impassioned oration. Several men responded with equal eloquence and after about a half-hour of speeches, they disbanded. It seems that one of the shepherds, who had rented a church-owned small house, was refusing to pay the rent asked of him. He had been threatened with eviction but had not responded even to this. The priest had called the men of the community together to try to get backing for his decision to evict the man. The authority was granted him on that rainy Sunday, but the shepherd finally agreed to go part way toward meeting the demand and continued to live in the house.

Religious Feast Days

If the formal organization of church affairs involves village-wide action or concern only in times of crisis, certain feasts and ceremonies of the Greek Orthodox Church certainly provide a focus of interest for the entire village at regular intervals during the year. The most conspicuous of these is the sequence of events by which the villagers celebrate Easter. The Sunday before Lent begins is the particular day which starts the holiday observances in Vasilika. After church services, children ran about in the morning trying to throw powdered soot at each other and at unsuspecting adults. Later in the day, the children and unmarried men and women dressed in costumes in preparation for the arrival of the musicians—this time there were a clarinetist, a violinist, and the player of a *sanduri* (dulcimer). Some boys and girls dressed as animals and their trainers went around in groups trying to frighten the very small children or just laughing at their own antics. The young people dressed themselves as gypsies, and some of the boys put on women's clothes and walked around with mincing steps and female gestures, while some of the girls donned men's clothes and twirled false moustaches. Throughout the afternoon and early evening the musicians sat in the *aghora* and the young people and their elders danced in the space between the two coffeehouses, as virtually all the rest of the village population sat and watched. Some spectators sat at the coffeehouse tables drinking beer or soda; others brought chairs from home to sit along the walls of the houses near the *aghora*. Still others watched from second-story windows overlooking the area. All the spectators sat quietly and without expression. Those who danced paid the musicians and occasionally the watchers would proffer a glass of *ouzo* (anise liqueur) to the male dancers and to the musicians.

The dances themselves were the most commonly known traditional round dances of the Greek countryside: the *kalamatyanos, sirtos,* and *tsamikos,* danced in Vasilika by both men and women, but usually not at the same time. Men danced the *zembekikos* and the *khasapikos* as solos.

On this occasion, and on any other when musicians came to the village, the women of some of the more sophisticated families joined their male relatives sitting around the small coffeehouse tables.

In the evening, several families joined together for a meat-eating feast, after which bonfires were lit in different sections of the village; this time the adults joined in the carnival spirit of practical jokes and danced and sang in the security of their own neighborhoods until early morning. The next day is "Clean Monday." Many of the villagers visited Kifisokhori, which has a carnival with a float competition on this day. In 1956, the winning float was a huge replica of the Trojan horse.

The events of Holy Week, with their culmination in the feasting and dancing on Easter Sunday, are from the villagers' point of view the most important time of the year. They anticipate *to Paskha* all the rest of the year; the women in particular asked about how Americans celebrated Easter more frequently than they asked about any other American custom, and whenever any general discussion of different customs came up, the women would spontaneously start describing Holy Week. Not the least of the reasons for the anticipation of Easter is that it is a spring festival and the villagers wait impatiently for spring. They look forward to the warmth of the sun after the cold and rainy winter, and they speak with affection of the beauty of the wild flowers which cover the hillsides in early spring.

During Holy Week in 1956, Maundy Thursday services began at 8:40 in the evening. Men and boys, as well as some women who rarely attended Sunday mass, appeared for the service, and on Good Friday and Easter Sunday virtually the entire village population, except for tiny infants and those who had to care for them, was present. By Thursday evening, relatives of the villagers from the surrounding villages and towns and from Athens had begun to arrive and to appear at the church. Just as on ordinary Sundays, the church filled gradually as the service progressed. Older men stood at the stalls up front, and several elderly women and pregnant women sat on chairs which were brought in for them and were placed in the back of the church in the woman's section. Women visitors were offered chairs; some accepted, some did not. Two of the village women got tired at one point and squatted on the floor, but as usual, the children, the younger men, and almost all the girls and women stood throughout. The service lasted until 11:00. In the course of it, there was considerable restlessness and low-voiced conversation among the men and giggling among the girls. But at the culmination of the service, when the image of Jesus on the Cross was brought from behind the screened altar and placed in the center of the church, there was complete quiet.

Many of the villagers can recite or chant the portions of the New Testament which are read as part of the Holy Week services, and do so under their breath—really only to themselves, since the priest and the chanters sing the chants aloud. Even among these villagers, however, very few have a literal understanding of the text, for it is in New Testament Greek, which is a generalized form of Eastern Mediterranean Greek developed in the last centuries of the pagan and early centuries of the Christian era. It is therefore about as different from the contemporary demotic Greek spoken in the village as Chaucerian English is from Modern English. Nevertheless, all the villagers know the main outlines of the New Testament depicting the crucifixion, death, and resurrection of Christ, and know which portions are being sung and symbolically re-enacted at each of the Holy Week services.

The villagers say that on Good Friday no one should work either in the fields or in the house, but these prohibitions were not strictly adhered to. In the morning, small boys went from house to house crying, *"Mavros in o uranos,"* "The sky is black," and they were given money or eggs. Meanwhile, the girls of the village worked inside the church covering with wild flowers the sedan-chairlike wooden frame in which an oil painting of Jesus on his bier was to be carried around the village that night. The frame and the icon together are called the *epitafios.* The girls seemed thoroughly to enjoy the morning's work, and they laughed, giggled, jostled each other, and called out orders. Occasionally they sang as they worked. It appeared also as if they were taking particular joy in being inside the church with no men to restrain them. They took turns sprawling over the stalls in which, as females, they rarely sat during a service. They also went up to the chanters' stand and recited some of the cantilations which were to be sung that night—the girls can follow the liturgy only silently during the course of the actual service. Some of the younger girls even dared each other to go behind the panel to the altar, a place forbidden to females, but none actually did. They seemed uneasy and were even frightened at the suggestion.

The church bell rang at 2:20 that afternoon. The priest, with one of the chanters and his son, performed the service in the course of which he brought the icon from behind the altar, covered it with a white cloth and placed it in its bower. In accordance with the symbolic re-enactment of the event, only the women and girls (and a few schoolboys) were in the church at the time. Once the icon was in place and strewn with flowers, the priest and then the children went up to kiss it. The priest explained that it should be done slowly and deliberately, exactly as it was done for the dead in the village funeral rituals.

Good Friday services began that night at 9:00. At 11:00 the *epitafios* was carried out of the church by four boys. These marched in procession with the *epitafios* behind boys carrying the *lavara* (standards). Behind the *epitafios* walked the priest and the chanters. The rest of the villagers followed holding candles to light the way as the *epitafios* was carried around the entire village. As the bells of the three village churches pealed, and the children chanted *"Enas ine o theos"* and *"Panayia dhespina,"* "God is one" and "Our Lady, the All Holy One," the villagers picked their way carefully over the stones and ruts as they climbed the hillside, circled the whole settlement, and climbed down again on the other side. When the procession reached the church door once more, the boys held the bier high so that the returning congregation passed into the church under it. The service was over shortly after midnight.

On Holy Saturday, sweet Easter breads with red eggs inside were displayed, other eggs were dyed red, last minute finishing touches were given to Easter clothes and last house-cleaning chores were completed. Some people slaughtered the Easter lamb on Saturday, others waited until Sunday. In the meantime, field chores went on as usual. Everyone rested for a few hours, from about 9:00 Saturday night until the Easter Sunday services began shortly after midnight. These lasted until 4:00 in the morning, with two periods of climax. The first occurred when all the lights in the church were put out and the priest kindled the new light. The boys rushed up to see who could be the first to light his own candle from that of the priest's. They said the winner would be the first of the boys to be married. The rest of the congregation then lit its candles from the priest's, or from each other's if they got impatient waiting to reach the priest. The second climax was, of course, the moment when, with the entire congregation standing outside the church, the priest announced, *"Khristos anesti,"* "Christ is risen," and the boys set off firecrackers.

After the service, people took a short nap, because by 6:00 in the morning, final preparations for Easter dinner would start. As has already been indicated, families joined with neighbors or relatives to eat the spit-roasted Easter lamb. Visiting relatives moved about to greet the villagers they knew. Baptisms, which had been arranged for the afternoon because prospective godparents enjoyed visiting the village at Easter, took place in the church, and the white baptismal clothes of the babies added sparkle to all the Easter finery. After an afternoon service in the church of St. Nicholas, the musicians came, settled in the *aghora,* and dancing began. But fewer villagers participated in either the dancing or the watching than at Carnival, because people preferred to spend more time at home with their visiting relatives. Nevertheless, a good crowd kept the *aghora* musicians occupied until eight in the evening, after which singing could be heard here and there about the village. The next day some of the young boys claimed to have been up singing half the night.

The description just given is only a brief outline of the main events and lacks many details of the village's celebration of Easter. My purpose in including it here is to illustrate the point that Carnival and Holy Week are times at which the Greek Orthodox rites and the accompanying customs provide activities in which all villagers participate at the same time and within the confines of Vasilika. Even under these circumstances, however, the visiting relatives act as a countervailing centrifugal force, pulling each family in the direction of its extra-village interests, as they use the holiday visit as an opportunity for family consultations on the problems of the coming year, and as the visitors tell of their lives in other villages, in towns, and in the cities.

Vasilika's *paniyiri,* the feast day of its patron saints, St. Cosmos and St. Damian, on the 1st of July, is another occasion when a religious event is celebrated by the entire village and draws visitors to the community. Other holy days and Sunday masses do not draw all the villagers together in the same way. School children are the most faithful communicants for regular Sunday mass; a small proportion of women and girls attend regularly, but the rest of the inhabitants appear to attend sporadically, as they please. During periods of heavy agricultural work, mass may be omitted on a Sunday. For the most part, individuals and families, rather than the village, are the units for participation in the formal religious activity of the settlement.

The Villagers as Greeks

To summarize the situation, the formal organization of the village community, the *kinotis,* provides neither autonomy in village affairs nor a unified structure. Decisions made by the village leaders are subject to approval by outside political authorities. Governmental, commercial, religious, and educational activities, although ultimately controlled in Athens, function through different organizational channels. The unity that might be achieved by overlapping personnel in a village as small as Vasilika is not, in fact, achieved because each of the formal divisions has its own leadership. Some degree of concurrence exists, however, as a result of the tendency for the leaders in each of these spheres, except the governmental, to remain relatively permanent. The priest has been the religious leader of the community for a generation, the former secretary of the council had been in office for twenty years, the school teacher has been there for ten years, and so on. Nevertheless, officials who want to persuade Vasilika's population to some new course of action know that they cannot succeed by persuading the formal leaders only, or even the influential older men only, but must convince each head of a family, as well, if they are to get widespread compliance.

It would seem as though the formal organization of the village, and the family activities which so often lead out of the village and separate the interests of each family from those of others in the settlement, prevent the life-long daily associations of the men of the village from producing a driving force for enthusiastic joint action for village-wide goals. Nor does the system of voluntary, impermanent dyadic contracts between individuals produce any large groups with a sense of solidarity. As the foregoing has shown, then, there are activities which focus the attention of all the villagers but there is little active village-wide cooperation for village enterprises.

Yet this situation seems to conflict with the professed attitude of Vasilika's inhabitants toward their village and region. The villagers speak of Vasilika in the way Greeks from other villages speak of their home communities. A man or woman's *patridha,* that is, his village of origin in this context (*patridha* may mean Greece as one's nation of origin in contrast with other nations), is always recommended as a place to visit. People frequently mentioned certain qualities of their home villages which were worthy of praise. The air and the water, they would say, are clean, in the sense of pure and sweet, and these characteristics, they thought, made the village a healthy place, and, by extension, potentially therapeutic for anyone. The people of one's own village were *endopyi* (home folks) in contrast to *kseni* (strangers), and the term *kseni* was used equally to refer to a man from Parori two miles away, and to us from the United States thousands of miles distant.

Kseni, people not living in Vasilika, were described as thieves and as inhospitable. We were consistently told to lock our automobile in other villages, and also consistently told that it was not necessary to do so in Vasilika. Indeed, both with respect to other villages and within Vasilika itself, a distrust of others was most frequently expressed by saying that the villagers in question were thieves, and it was an accusation not meant lightly. On two occasions before we understood the situation, when we mislaid a pair of scissors and some clothespins, we asked the family with which we lived whether any one of them had seen the lost items. The family construed the question as an accusation that they had stolen the items from us, and it took several hours of reassuring conversation to convince them that we had meant nothing of the kind. Evidence suggests that an individual's or family's *filotimo* would be considered severely damaged if they stole from a stranger to whom hospitality had been offered; in fact, such thefts are very rare in any Greek village. Within Vasilika itself, there was some petty filching now and then, but it did not occur on the scale one would have expected from the frequent references to theft and thieving in conversation.

The inhospitality of people in other places was a frequent topic of conversation at the homes of those celebrating name days. A man could always raise a laugh by describing the ludicrously meager food and drink provided at a wedding or name day celebration he had attended at another village. Usually in response to any questions about the occurrence in Vasilika of deviant behavior, or of some form of discord, or of some moral transgression, the villagers began by making a general statement of denial. Such things happened in other villages, they would say, but not in Vasilika.

It would seem from the foregoing that Vasilika's population did, indeed, identify itself with the village as an entity. Vasilika is their *patridha,* and it must be thought to have good qualities, I believe, because the village's qualities reflect on its inhabitants both in their status as individuals and as families. Pride in the village, then, may be an extension of pride in oneself or one's family, and the functional consequences for village-wide enterprises of the existence of such pride depend on the strength of the competing sources of satisfaction.

In Vasilika, since farms may be maintained by the labor of the elementary family with only periodic requirements for a larger labor force, since sons and daughters leave the village and yet maintain relationships with those still in Vasilika, and since individuals can expect to give and to receive protection from their families, the forces leading toward either independence or family solidarity would appear to be strong enough to leave little energy for village-centered activities as a method of augmenting self-esteem. Nevertheless, the village as an entity constitutes a permanent potential source of satisfaction for its inhabitants, and now and then, under certain circumstances, the village itself becomes the primary object of loyalty for its population and commands some sacrifice. The boundary dispute with Parori was such an occasion for Vasilika. Moreover, any individual can, if he wishes, use his energies when he occupies an official position to gain improvements for the village as a means of enhancing his own self-esteem and of gaining the respect of the villagers, as long as he does not do so at the expense of his own children. The people of Vasilika are entirely willing to enjoy and to speak proudly of the electricity, or the piped water, or the better roads in Vasilika, once they have obtained them, even if they are not always willing to work together to achieve the improvements.

But Vasilika, as a village, must compete with another focus of loyalty for its inhabitants besides the family: Greekness itself—and the Greek nation as a political entity. The villagers' awareness of and pride in their Greekness is profound. In 1956 when we were questioning the children as to what they wanted to be when they grew up, several boys answered that they hoped God would let them grow strong and sturdy so that they could be good soldiers and go to "Fight for Cyprus." Moreover, the villagers associate certain qualities with Greek ethnicity: the desire for political independence and the willingness to fight for it against overwhelming odds—they cite the evidence of the ancient Greek Battle of Marathon, of the revolution against the Turks, and of the refusal to give in to the Italians during World War II; the love of freedom in all spheres to the point of unwillingness to take orders from anyone— "Twelve Greeks, thirteen Captains," they say; cleverness and guile—they cite Odysseus and the success of Greek merchants the world over; the love of talk and of political conversation in particular—they cite Aristotle's comments on man as a political animal and illustrate his point by referring to the coffeehouse talk in Vasilika; the love of adventure, of *peripetyes,* of risk—they cite their preference for the Odyssey over the Iliad because the Odyssey has more vicissitudes; the hospitality extended to strangers often at the expense of the family—they cite *Ksenios Zefs* (Zeus, the patron of strangers) and the sheltering of individuals during the German occupation. This list does not exhaust the Greek qualities the villagers assign themselves. But the qualities and the examples given are included to show that the people of Vasilika think of themselves as Greeks with a set of ethnic characteristics which they believe they have shared with the inhabitants of the country in historical continuity from classical Greek times, through Byzantium, into the present.

For a volume on a modern Greek village to refer in the first chapter to ancient Greek tragedy and to end with a reference to the sense of kinship the villagers have with the ancient Greeks is peculiarly fitting. Although the classical Greeks are by no means in the forefront of the villagers' consciousness, and although their understanding of the details of the classical age is incomplete, the knowledge that "Greece brought light to the world" contributes to the villagers' faith in their own ability to develop themselves and their country. The people of Vasilika are proud of being Greeks and they want very much to achieve *proödhos* (progress) for their families, for their village, and for the glory that is Greece.

Glossary

Greek terms given below are transliterated approximately according to the system used by Kahane, Kahane, and Ward, 1945, which is also employed throughout the text, except for certain geographical names.

AGHORA: Market place, central square

DHIMOTIKI: Demotic, the popular spoken form of the modern Greek language

DROPI: Shame

FILOTIMO: Sense of honor, amour-propre

GHAMBROS: Son-in-law; a man who has married into the speaker's family

GLIGHORA: Quickly

KHORTA: Green plants, growing wild, and used as vegetables

KINOTIS: A community as a governmental unit

KSENOS (plural, KSENI): Stranger; foreigner, outlander

KUMBAROS: Godparent at baptism; sponsor at marriage

LIRA (plural, LIRES): Gold sovereign; coined gold

NIFI: Daughter-in-law; a woman who has married into the speaker's family

OKA (plural, OKADHES): A weight equal to 2.8 pounds

PANIYIRI: An annual festival at which a village or town celebrates its patron saint's day

PATRIDHA: Native country; place of birth

PITA: Kind of pie

PRIKA: Dowry

RETSINA: Resinated wine

RUKHA: Clothing; trousseau

SALONI: Parlor, ceremonial room

SOGHAMBROS: A man who has come to live in the house of his wife's family

STREMA (plural, STREMATA): A quarter-acre

VASANO (usually plural, VASANA): Trial, tribulation, trouble

References Cited

ANDROMEDAS, JOHN, 1957, Greek Kinship Terms in Everyday Use. *American Anthropologist,* 59: 1086-1088.

ANTONAKAKI, KALLINIKI DENDRINOU, 1955, *Greek Education.* New York: Teachers College, Columbia University.

FOSTER, GEORGE M., 1961, The Dyadic Contract: A Model for the Social Structure of a Mexican Peasant Village. *American Anthropologist,* 63: 1173-1192.

FRIEDL, ERNESTINE, 1958, Hospital Care in Provincial Greece. *Human Organization,* 16: 24-27.

———, 1959a, The Role of Kinship in the Transmission of National Culture to Rural Villages in Mainland Greece. *American Anthropologist,* 61: 30-38.

———, 1959b, Dowry and Inheritance in Modern Greece. *Transactions of the New York Academy of Sciences,* 22: 49-54.

The Greek Civil Code, edited by G. A. Babaratou, Athens. (In Greek only)

KAHANE, HENRY and RENEE, and RALPH L. WARD, 1945, *Spoken Greek.* New York: Holt, Rinehart and Winston.

LEE, DOROTHY D., 1953, Greece. In *Cultural Patterns and Technical Change,* edited by Margaret Mead. Unesco, pp. 77-114.

LEVY, HARRY L., 1956, Property Distribution by Lot in Present Day Greece. *Transactions of the American Philological Association,* 87: 42-46.

MILLER, HENRY, 1950, *The Colossus of Maroussi.* London: Penguin Books.

NEWBIGIN, MARION I., 1949, *Southern Europe: a Regional and Economic Geography of the Mediterranean Lands.* New York: Dutton, third revised edition.

SANDERS, IRWIN T., 1962, *Rainbow in the Rock: The People of Rural Greece.* Cambridge: Harvard University Press.

Recommended Reading

Most of the items among the references cited can be considered as recommended reading as well.

On Greece

DURRELL, LAWRENCE, 1957, *Bitter Lemons*. New York: Dutton.
> Comments of a sensitive writer on the Cyprus issue just before the independence of the island.

FORSTER, EDWARD S., 1941, *A Short History of Modern Greece 1821–1940*. London: Methuen.
> One of the few works of this kind available in English.

LEE, DOROTHY D., 1953, Greece. In *Cultural Patterns and Technical Change*, edited by Margaret Mead, Unesco, pp. 77-114.
> A full and perceptive discussion of Greek attitudes and values.

McNEILL, WILLIAM HARDY, 1957, *Greece: American Aid in Action 1947–1956*. New York: Twentieth Century Fund.
> An excellent analysis which includes much material on Greek social and economic conditions.

MEGAS, GEORGE A., 1958, *Greek Calendar Customs*. Athens: Press and Information Department, Prime Minister's Office.
> A useful, generalized description of customs associated with feasts and festivals.

SANDERS, IRWIN T., 1962, *Rainbow in the Rock: The People of Rural Greece*. Cambridge: Harvard University Press.
> An indispensable general description of a kind not previously available.

SWEET-ESCOTT, BICKHAM, 1954, *Greece, a Political and Economic Survey 1939–1953*. New York: Royal Institute of International Affairs.
> Fine analysis of World War II period.

Of the many books by foreign travelers or residents in Greece in recent times, the following, although essentially accounts of personal reactions to the country, include valuable descriptions of the land and the people.

ANDREWS, KEVIN, 1959, *The Flight of Ikaros.* Boston: Houghton Mifflin.

DURRELL, LAWRENCE, 1960, *Prospero's Cell* and *Reflections on a Marine Venus.* New York: Dutton.

LEE, C. P., 1957, *Athenian Adventure.* New York: Knopf.

MILLER, HENRY, 1950, *The Colossus of Maroussi.* London: Penguin Books.

On the Concept of the Peasant

FITCHEN, JANET MATHEWS, 1961, Peasantry as a Social Type. In *Proceedings of the 1961 Annual Spring Meeting of the American Ethnological Society,* edited by Viola E. Garfield. Seattle: University of Washington Press, pp. 114–119.

FOSTER, GEORGE M., 1961, The Dyadic Contract: A Model for the Social Structure of a Mexican Peasant Village. *American Anthropologist,* 63: 1173–1192.

FOSTER, GEORGE M., et al., 1960–61, Interpersonal Relations in Peasant Society. *Human Organization,* 19: 174-184.

A lively debate on how best to describe peasant personality.

REDFIELD, ROBERT, 1956, *Peasant Society and Culture.* Chicago: University of Chicago Press.

This book has rapidly become a classic and is indispensable reading for students of peasant cultures.

WOLF, ERIC R., 1955, Types of Latin American Peasantry. *American Anthropologist,* 57: 452-471.

A provocative classification of peasant communities the usefulness of which is by no means limited to Latin America.

The following two articles attempt to define some characteristics of the emerging industrial societies in which a large proportion of the population still has rural occupations.

CASAGRANDE, JOSEPH B., 1959, Some Observations on the Study of Intermediate Societies. In *Intermediate Societies, Social Mobility, and Communication,* edited by Verne F. Ray, Seattle: University of Washington Press, pp. 1-10. (See also comments by A. Lesser in the volume.)

PITKIN, DONALD S., 1959, The Intermediate Society: A Study in Articulation. In *Intermediate Societies, Social Mobility, and Communication,* edited by Verne F. Ray, Seattle: University of Washington Press, pp. 14-19.